A Quick Guide To Stock Market Crashes

Understand Crashes With Examples, Look For Signs And Prepare Strategies

By Simon Milgard

Disclaimer

All examples and explanations are strictly for demonstrative purposes only. They are not recommendations to buy or sell certain securities. Please do the appropriate research and consult a certified financial professional if necessary before you trade and invest. Some methods discussed in the book may not be suitable for everybody depending on individual ability and/or risk tolerance.

Copyright © 2020

Table of Contents

Introduction..5
Chapter 1..6
Defining A Stock Market Crash...6
    Figure 1.0..6
    Figure 1.1..7
Chapter 2..9
Examining Common Characteristics In Stock Market Crash Examples.....................................9
    Figure 2.0..9
    Figure 2.1..10
    Figure 2.2..10
    Figure 2.4..11
    Figure 2.5..11
     Figure 2.6...12
    Figure 2.7..13
    Figure 2.8..13
    Figure 2.9..14
    Figure 2.10..15
    Figure 2.11..16
    Figure 2.12..17
    Figure 2.13..18
    Figure 2.14..19
    Figure 2.15..19
    Figure 2.16..20
    Figure 2.17..21
    Figure 2.18..21
    Figure 2.19..22
    The Stock Market vs. The Economy...22
    Figure 2.20..24
    Figure 2.21..25
    Figure 2.22..26
    Figure 2.23..27
    Figure 2.24..28
    Figure 2.25..29
    Figure 2.26..30
    Figure 2.27..31
    Flash Crashes..31
    Figure 2.28..32
    Figure 2.29..33
     Figure 2.30...34
Chapter 3..36
Causes And Contributing Factors In Stock Market Crashes..36
    Figure 3.0..36
    Figure 3.1..37
    Figure 3.2..38

- Figure 3.3..38
- Figure 3.4..39
- Figure 3.5..40
- Figure 3.6..40
- Figure 3.7..42
- Figure 3.8..42
- Figure 3.9..43
- Figure 3.10..44
- Figure 3.11..45
- Figure 3.12..46
- Figure 3.13..46
- Figure 3.14..47
- Figure 3.15..49
- Figure 3.16..50
  - Figure 3.17..52
  - Figure 3.18..54
  - Figure 3.19..54

Chapter 4..55
Stock Market Crash Strategies...55
- Figure 4.0..55
- Strategy 1...56
- Strategy 2...57
- Strategy 3...58
- Strategy 4...59
- Strategy 5...60
- Strategy 6...61
- Strategy 7...62
- Strategy 8...63
- Strategy 9...63
- Strategy 10...64

Introduction

Before even trying to determine what a stock market crash is let's save lots of time and effort by abbreviating "stock market crash" as SMC. "SMCs" will be used to refer to this term in the plural form. After outlining the definition of what SMCs are, there will be a series of real chart examples that put theoretical ideas into real world context. A series of case studies also serves to present common characteristics of SMCs no matter the place, time, or market. In other words the core characteristics of stock market crashes will be outlined and allow for greater chances of identifying SMCs regardless of the place, time, or market. The examples used in this book will of course get old over time but the main characteristics of SMCs they highlight are invaluable for examining SMCs in the past or the future. After a firm understanding of the core chart characteristics of SMCs a discussion of fundamental factors contributing to SMCs will be presented followed by a series of strategies for falling markets.

For more on trading, charting, and the markets visit www.ascencore.com/

Chapter 1

Defining A Stock Market Crash

Figure 1.0

SMCs are essentially price drops on a large scale. That means it is mainly a matter of defining the characteristics of a price drop that would qualify it to be an SMC. Thus the following 3 essential questions are to be asked when trying to determine whether a drop in the stock market is an SMC.

- How big is the drop?
- How long does the drop last?
- How fast does price drop?

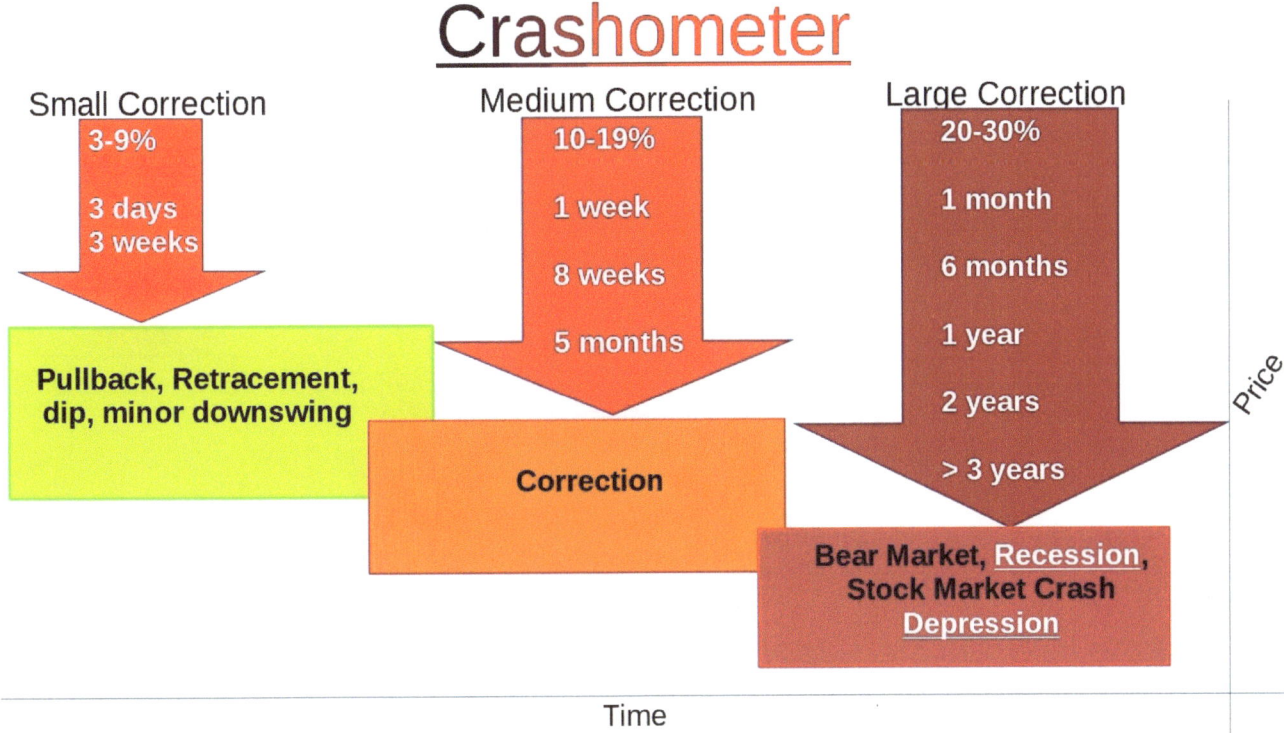

Figure 1.1

The above diagram concisely categorizes price drops and when they can begin to be considered crashes. This can be applied to a whole stock market, a sector in the stock market, or a single individual stock. These thresholds based on the 3 essential questions mentioned before, are what largely determine when the word crash can appropriately be used when referring to a drop in price in the stock market.

The word "correction" is often used to describe the first two categories with drops below 20% in less than a 6 month period. However "correction" is also used for drops of a greater magnitude and length of time. It is less common but it does happen and usually in the context and from the perspective of long term investing that looks at events over the spans of years and decades rather than weeks and months.

The "bear" minimum (pun intended) for an SMC is a 20% drop lasting for at least 6 months. Anything significantly greater begins to shift towards full scale depressions which are extremely rare but long lasting in duration and significant in the lost value in stocks. There is no widely agreed upon set of values for when a recession becomes a depression. The most important note here is the more agreed upon threshold of at least a 20% drop lasting for at least 6 months, as the minimum needed to define a stock market to be undergoing an SMC, or a particular stock or sector to be undergoing a bear market. Anything more than this minimum criteria becomes a matter of perspective and preference as to when a recession becomes interchangeable with bear market and other analogous terms like downturn or slump. Eventually a point is reached when all those terms are reused but in a tone that emphasizes a larger and longer lasting drop such as strong bear market or long lasting downturn. After that the word depression is used and some may argue it is when a drop of at least 50% lasts for at least one year. In any case popular culture often refers to anything as an SMC starting from a recession. Though in more technical terms "correction" is just a fancy way of referring to a drop of any magnitude. It is just more commonly associated with the first two categories on the diagram. Thus the diagram is almost like a sizing diagram similar to things such as sizing clothes in small, medium, and large, or difficulty of a test or game as easy, medium, and hard. Except in this case the simple 3 category scale is used to describe the approximate separation of small corrections which commonly get called other names such as; pullbacks, retracements, dips, and minor downswings. Then "correction" as a term in the stock market is most commonly associated with the 2nd category of "drop" also called "corrections" which are between 10% and 19% and lasting anywhere from a week up to 5 months.

As a side note the word "correction" is most commonly used to refer to the second category because that is usually a drop that is large enough and long enough to stabilize a market that has risen too much, but a the same time not drop, or "correct" too much so as to maintain a more balanced market that is neither overextended too high or oversold too low. In effect the medium category is deemed to be an optimal re balancing of stock markets to allow for sustainable periods of rising and periods to relieve selling pressure so the proverbial "bubble" doesn't inflate and burst with a pent up delay in overdue selling.

In terms of frequency small drops/corrections are very common and even occur during the strongest bullish up trends, they can occur anywhere from once a week to even once a month(if it is a very strong up trending market). Then medium drops/corrections are naturally less common but are still fairly normal to witness. They may occur in a range from every month or two to even less than 4 times a year(once again in cases of strong up trending markets). Lastly large drops/corrections in SMC territory take place at less defined intervals. Though it is commonly agreed that at a minimum the stock market undergoes an SMC approximately once a decade. This is debatable but in general stock markets often see the minimum threshold of a 20% drop lasting for at least 6 months being crossed every 5-10 years. Large scale SMCs reaching historic depression status are accordingly even rarer and may not happen for decades. As well when a market is on a strong up trend for over 5 years and still doesn't cross the threshold for an SMC to take place it is still normal to see 20% drops that last for a short duration usually well under 6 months, often resulting in short lived periods of panic and high volatility.

Lastly it is also important to remember this is only a conceptual diagram. When we look at examples as is so often the case in real live markets, situations are much more fluid. In fact sometimes not all 3 elements will be met to neatly categorize a market to strictly be in one defined category. In some cases the market will decline enough to meet the threshold of one category but the duration of the drop doesn't last long enough. Simply remember that diagrams like this are always useful to conceptualize ideas like SMCs but when applied in reality they are best thought of as approximate guidelines to mark the approximate boundaries set out by dynamic criteria such as that of the magnitude, duration, and rate of falling stock prices. Moreover there is always the matter of personal perspective and preference for terminology, meaning these are also approximate definitions and terms. As is so often the case traders and investors will use words and phrases slightly differently depending on their perspectives and preference. Though overall the most agreed upon and commonly used terms and criteria have been outlined.

Chapter 2

Examining Common Characteristics In Stock Market Crash Examples

Figure 2.0

While the exact combination of fundamental causes behind SMCs differ to varying degrees from crash to crash, they still have some core characteristics that remain virtually constant. That is why it will be useful to examine SMCs of various magnitudes, across different markets and time periods. In doing so we can apply the "Crashometer" from figure 1.1 to real market contexts. Then before diving into the chart examples keep in mind a few key points that are vital for the effective examination of SMCs. In fact the following tips are useful for technical analysis of any charts no matter the market conditions, they are good practices for observing the nature of market behavior from a charting point of view. This can enhance understanding of technical analysis and compliment any fundamental analysis you may choose to use.

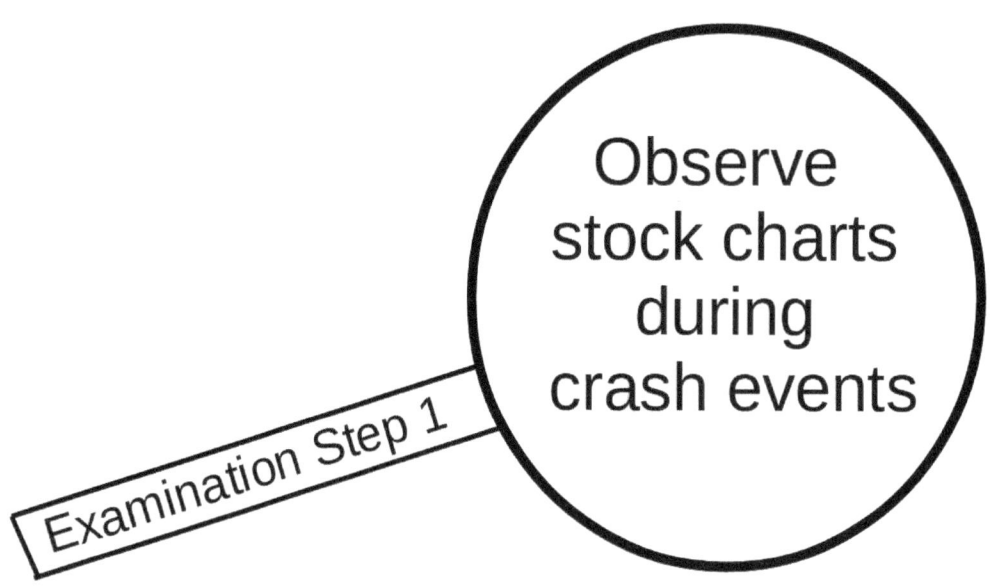

Figure 2.1

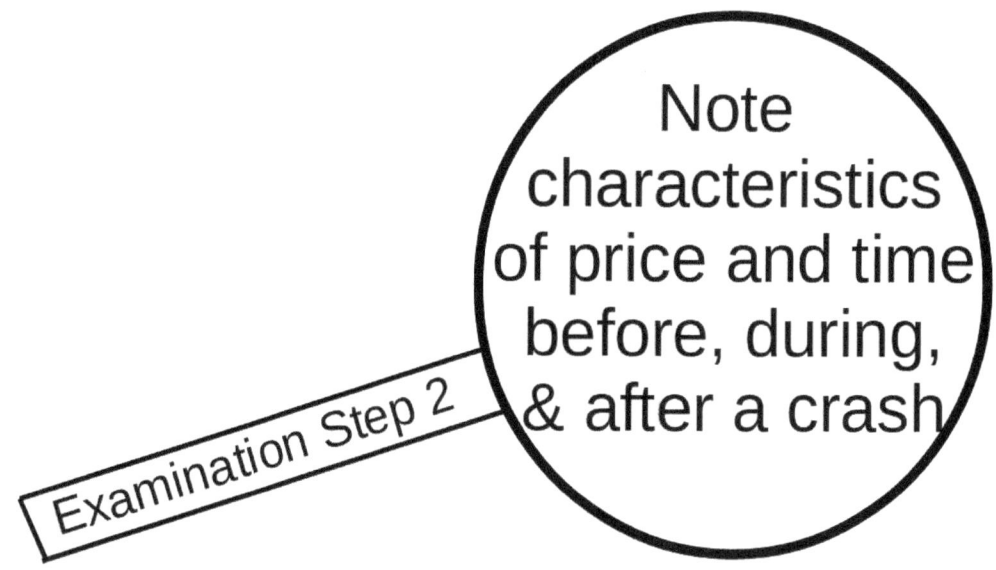

Figure 2.2

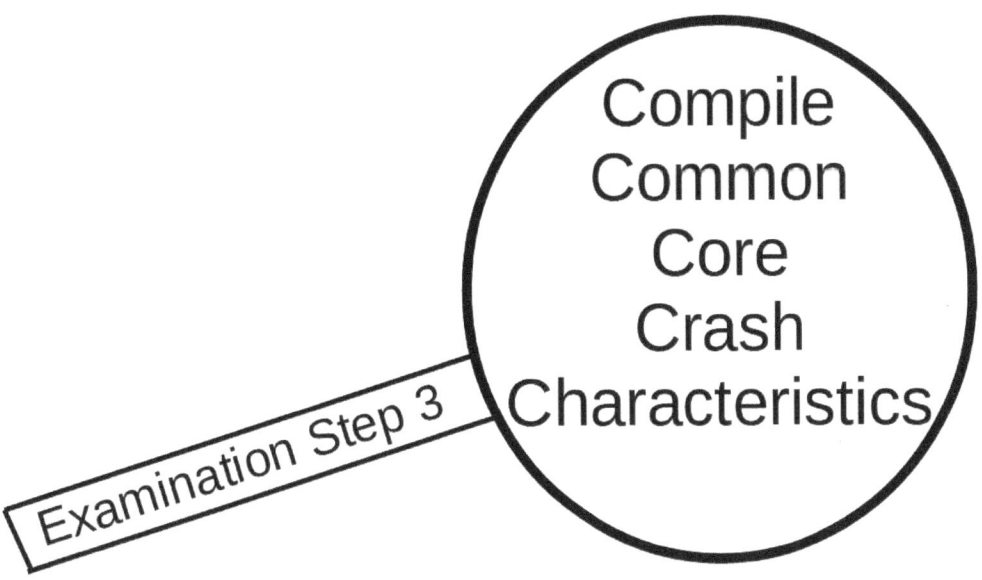

Figure 2.4

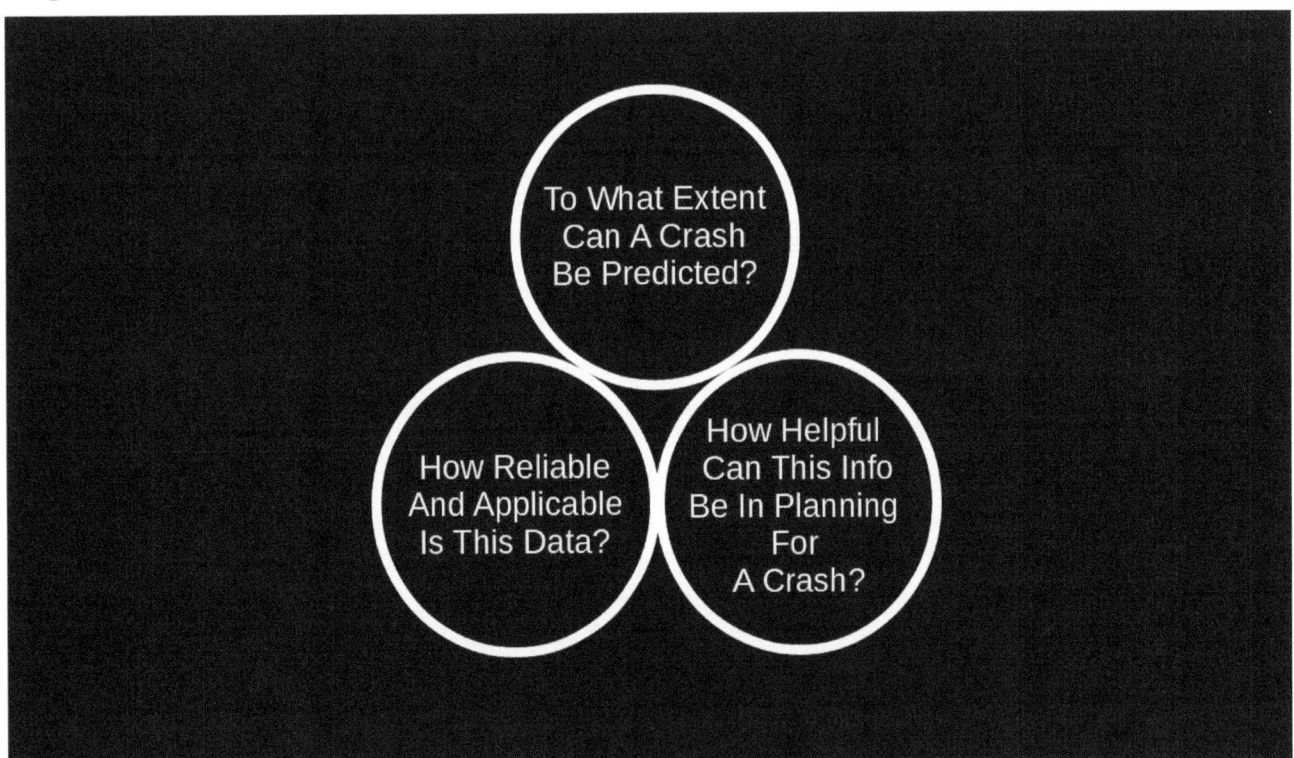

Figure 2.5

As for the study of any charting phenomenon it is important when applying the 3 steps of examination to ask additional questions about the degree of utility the examination reveals.

Up to this point everything has been more or less abstract since only conceptual features of SMCs have been described. Now this is when the proverbial "rubber hits the road," when ideas get put into practice.

Figure 2.6

A very straightforward uptrend is exhibited on a chart of the Dow Jones Industrial Average during the mid 2010s. However as mentioned before we are looking for key commonalities of price drops, and in particular price drops that meet the criteria to be called SMCs. Thus the first characteristic of SMCs displayed in figure 2.6 is an uptrend. More accurately it is to say a sustained uptrend precedes a major drop.

Overall it is quite a simple precursor to be aware of. Any chart no matter if it is an entire index like the Dow or an individual stock chart, the fact is the larger the rise in price and the longer price keeps rising without a sizable correction. Then the chances of a major drop entering minimum SMC territory are increased significantly. A common analogy used is to think of any chart as a rubber band. The more it gets pulled in one direction the more potential energy becomes available for a larger "rebound" or "pullback." This can apply to both rising bullish markets and falling bearish markets. In this case since we are discussing SMCs the hypothetical rubber band is being pulled up and up and up. Eventually this stores too much "selling pressure" (another common term). The result is an inevitable correction, and if the correction crosses the thresholds discussed in chapter 1 than it becomes an SMC, which is essentially a correction but in the longer term perspective and on a larger scale.

Figure 2.7

Continuing on wit the same Dow example we see the uptrend is sustained for so long due to regular healthy pullbacks. The market is often said to be in a "healthy" uptrend in cases like this because it never overextends too high due to the regular minor corrections.

Figure 2.8

Indeed this is very much the opposite of an SMC if you invert the minimum criteria. It is a rise of at least 20% lasting more than 6 months.

Figure 2.9

Towards October the Dow undergoes one of the largest drops it has experienced recently. The overall bull market is still healthy but in a short to medium term context of less than a year the stock market is overdue for a larger correction closer to a 10% drop. The Dow is a good first example not only because it is a classic index among one of the first stock market indices devised, but because it is also what most people are familiar with. Almost everyone has heard of the Dow either directly by following the chart and news, or indirectly by hearing or reading about it when skimming over some business/economic news while waiting for other news like weather and sports.

While there are other indices like the S&P 500 and Nasdaq the Dow still represented the American stock market quite well during this time period. In any case it is a good starting point to begin examination of core SMC features that can later be applied to more diverse and obscure charts that may not traditionally be at the forefront of public attention. After all core SMC features should be visible in virtually all contexts and we shall see that as we move beyond the traditional Dow Jones Industrial Average Index.

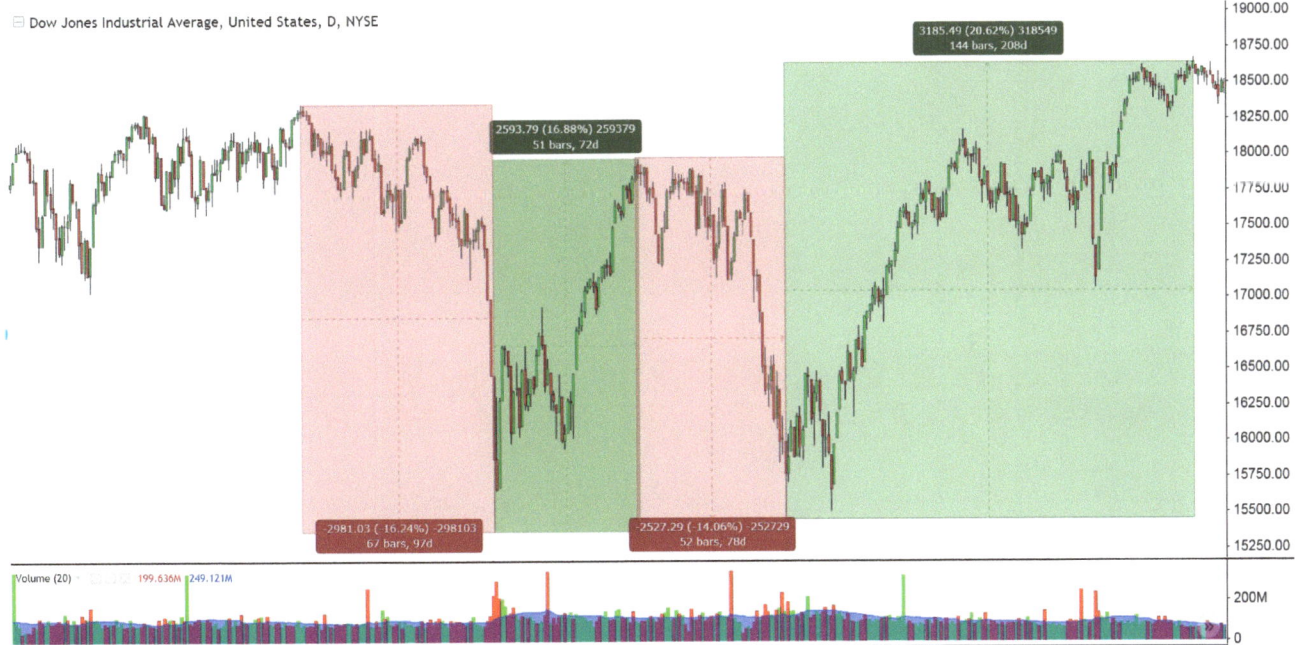

Figure 2.10

Over the next two years in the longer term context the Dow undergoes some more corrections closer to the common association of the word being used for 10-19% drops over a few weeks. In the short term the markets appear volatile and indeed during the 2015-2016 time period shown here it was common to call the Dow and stock markets around the world as going through "crazy times." Though given the sensible long term background we covered before, and with the benefit of hindsight such thinking was quite exaggerated.

Several things to note here from the start, beginning with the fact that drops are often faster and more volatile(in terms of wide daily price variations). This is in contrast to the recovery back up which is often characterized by slower and stabler moves.

The peaking high of the market down to the absolute low of the drop also tend to form natural ranges of support and resistance that will impact the market in the future. This is clearly demonstrated by the low 16000s to high 15000s range as a foundation of support for multiple bearish moves. As well the high 17000 to low 18000 range provided firm resistance to multiple bullish trends. Just like with any charts or market conditions these highs and lows are contentious areas that naturally attract attention and contention between buyers and sellers in the market. Since these are larger, longer term, and more influential reversal areas they will confine price in flatter ranges for longer periods of time. Then once these boundaries are eventually passed the market tends to advance smoothly towards new highs such as in this case. Conversely if the market breaks a lower supporting range it will often free fall further with ease for a time longer.

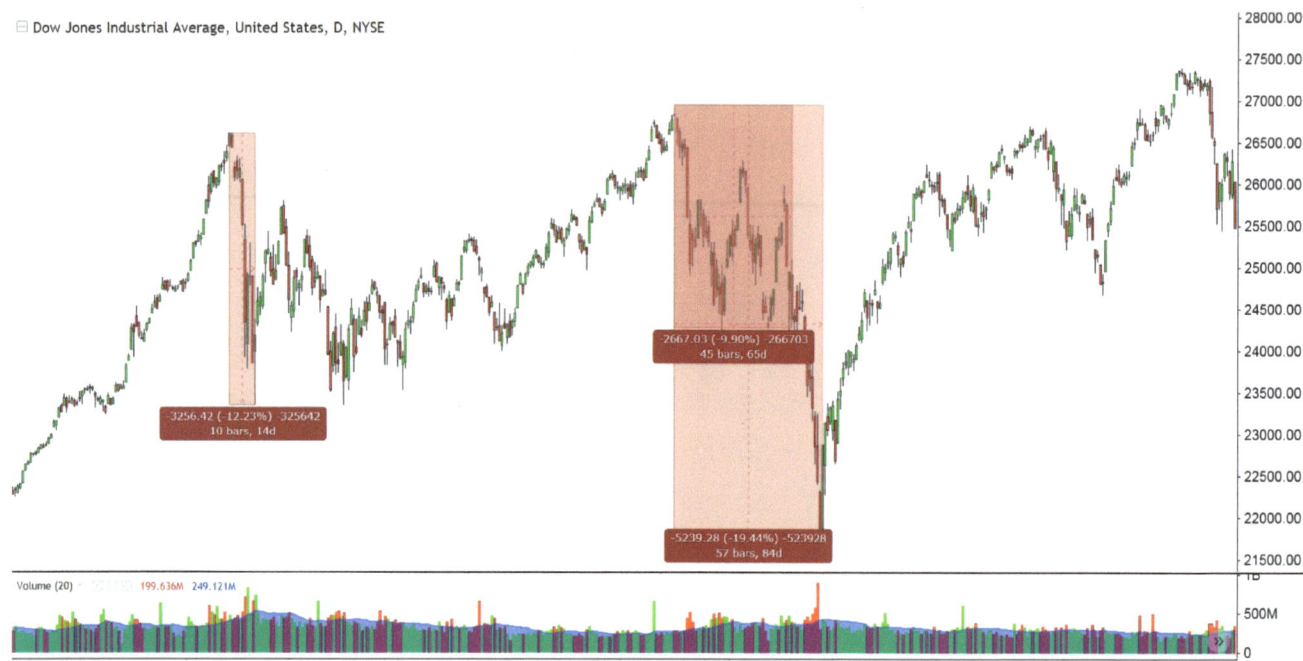

Figure 2.11

Another 2 years passes approximately and we see the Dow in more neutral ranges as it trades relatively flat from a long term perspective. However in the medium to short term context of less than a year the situation is more lively with constant reversals and more regular volatility resulting in large drops and rises from week to week becoming a more common sight during this time period.

First a new all time high is reached around the 26500 area after a short term over extension where the market rose on a near vertical climb on top of the longer term bullish context we observed earlier. Thus it was no surprise the market exhibited the core characteristic of an equally sharp move down in the short term following a very sharp peak. Then as seen before after the approximate 12.23% drop the market forms a very influential lower range. Although the first drop was indeed volatile it was a fairly standard event falling neatly into the category of a medium sized correction/drop.

Months later the Dow reaches a slightly newer all time high near the previous 26500 area following the characteristic slower bullish uptrend that was generally more stable than the initial sharp 12.23% drop. At that point the market began another downward reversal that has some key differences which relate back to the core SMC characteristics. Firstly since the rise to these new all time highs was more stable than the near vertical climb of the first correction, there was no one single sharp peak followed by a rapid fall. Instead a far more gradual downtrend formed with several smaller peaks that did surge down initially but after that a short to medium term supporting area formed and in total the drop was only around a 9.90% decline from the long term high to the initial low. Thus the downtrend in this second case started off as a small correction.

Then we see the utility of categorization as the market breaks below the temporary supporting range at a normal rapid pace that is to be expected after such a major lower boundary is passed. This results in nearly crossing the hypothetical line to be classified as a bear market and the smallest of SMCs.

However the Dow and the rest of the major stock market indices near this late 2018 time span didn't advance lower or stay lower for much longer. In fact we see the inverse. The short term sharp drop forms a sharp lower reversal point leading to an equally sharp incline back up on a near vertical climb. Quite the rebound and the exact opposite to the first instance with the volatile 12.23% drop. This again highlights the rubber band analogy and demonstrates the concept of over extension on the rising bullish and falling bearish sides of the market.

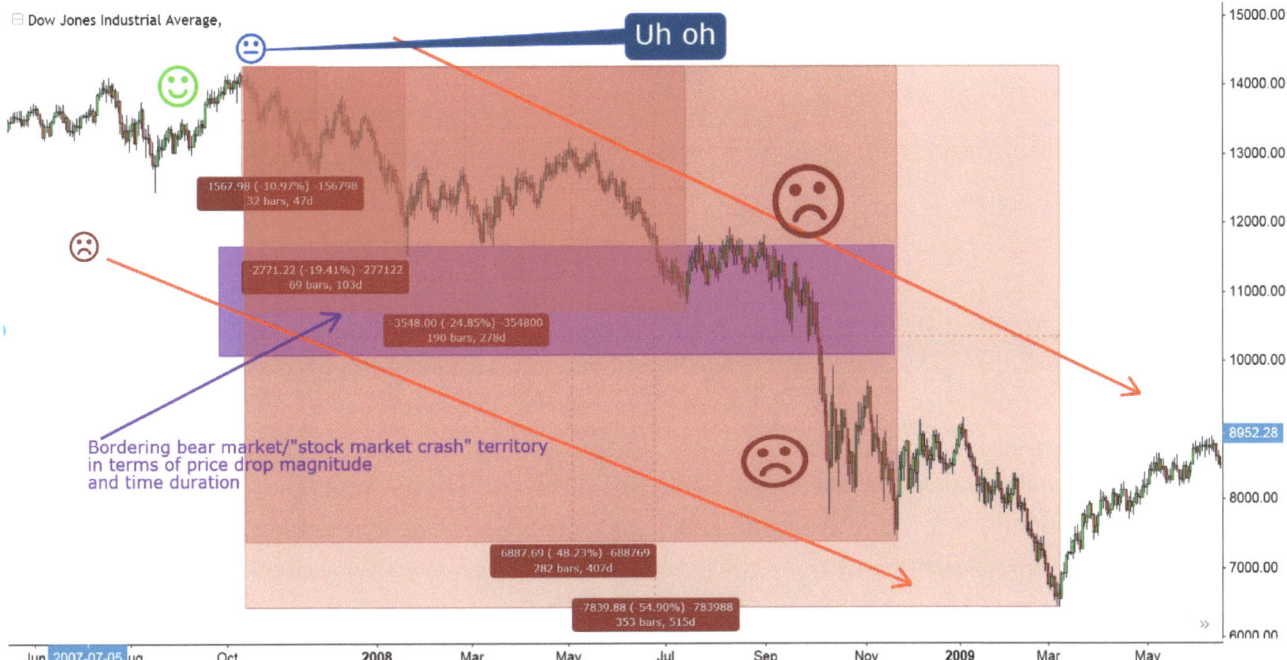

Figure 2.12

Using a chart of the Dow again we finally see an example of a full scale SMC that also outlines many of the key features already discussed during the previous examples of small to medium sized corrections. This is of course during the so called "great recession" from late 2007-2009.

At first it resembles the prior chart of the Dow almost a decade later in 2018. Initially there are several highs that gradually form lower a few volatile spikes drive the Dow down rapidly but overall the first stages of the drop are fairly gradual. It ends up with the Dow crossing the border from a small correction to medium sized correction towards the end of 2007 with consecutive lower highs and lower lows. A clear down trend forms with these declining downswing and minor upswing points. Soon the market is well in medium correction territory for several months to begin 2008. However it just barely avoids the 20% threshold until further in the year when a clear and decisive break lower firmly established the historic recession that was reflected in this SMC.

Along the way down we still see those classic support and resistance characteristics to demonstrate that even during such a massive decline stock markets can still slow down at key points and even reverse back up temporarily to definable resistance areas where they will often be driven back down at major high ranges from the past. Towards the end of 2008 the crash reaches a climax shortly after overcoming the low 11000 to 10000 support range to exhibit a normal free falling spike rapidly moving lower.

Figure 2.13

The Nasdaq Composite Index is more concentrated in the technology sector and as we all know the recession of 2008 mainly originated from the financial sector. However that being said the Nasdaq and the Dow as broad representations of the market still reflect the same general decline during the same approximate time span. Thus the fundamental causes of an SMC certainly can vary but the technical aspects in terms of the features seen on the charts, remains relatively consistent as they are core SMC characteristics.

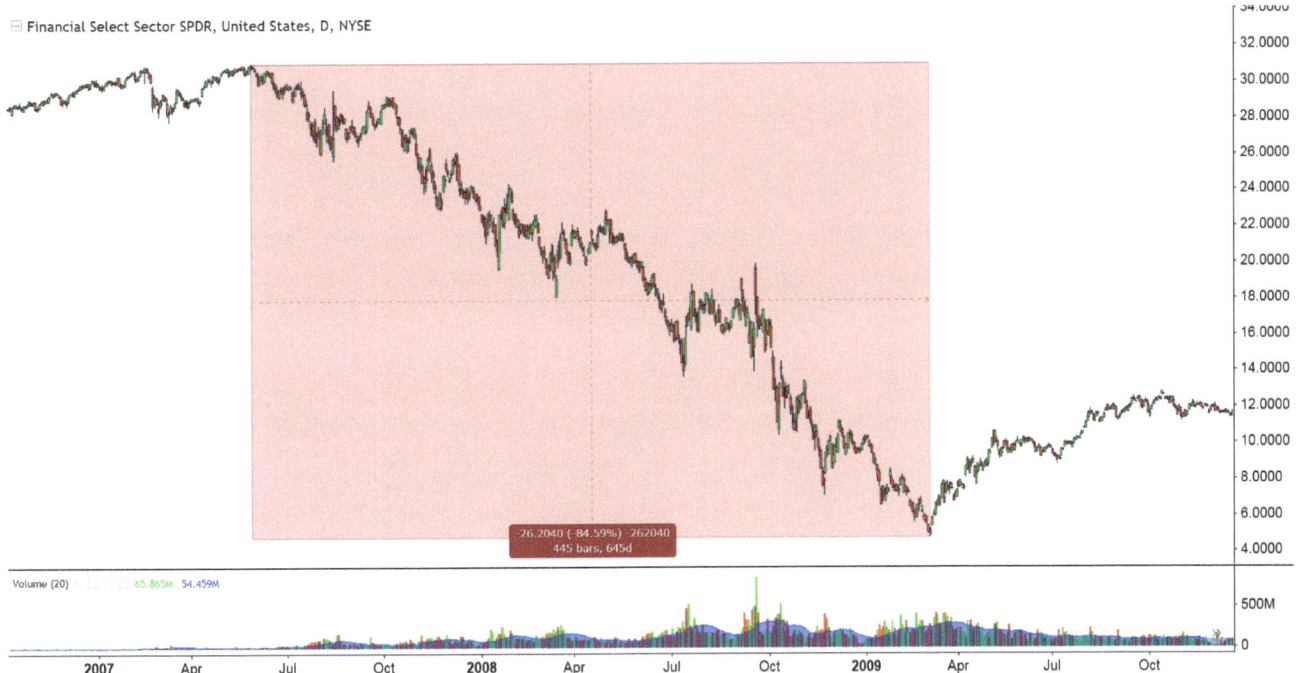

Figure 2.14

The XLF financial sector ETF obviously suffered more on all levels during the 2008 recession compared to broader market representations like the Dow or Nasdaq.

Figure 2.15

Normally broad representations of the market such as the Dow and Nasdaq experience SMCs to a lower degree. The same can be said for stock market sectors represented by ETFs and/or indices such as the XLF chart from figure 2.14. The main reason is because a broad representation of the market is composed of many individual stocks perhaps even 100s and 1000s of stocks. While an individual stock fully bears all the forces of market conditions. Bank of America was certainly a major bank within the financial sector during the late 2000s, coupled with the 2008 recession being a financial sector based decline. Then this one individual stock shouldered virtually the full effects of the crash in terms of the near complete loss of value in the stock price. This phenomenon can work the other way as individual stocks can rise significantly more than broader market indices or stock market sectors. Though in the context of SMCs this is realistically nearing the worst of the worst situations without a stock fully getting delisted and the underlying company going bankrupt.

From a charting standpoint the Bank of America(BAC) chart from figure 2.15 exhibits the same core SMC characteristics as seen on the previous charts that displayed broader representations of the market. However due to the factors discussed the BAC chart experienced everything to a much greater degree. The overall drop is of course larger. Volatility is much greater than the Nasdaq and Dow, and even XLF. Moreover the key price ranges are much wider due to the wider and stronger variations in downswings and upswings which generally appear and end at a much more rapid pace. In addition the peaks and rebounds are much sharper as evidenced by the many frequent and quick reversals on the way down.

Figure 2.16

To further reinforce the application of key SMC features in real live markets the Nasdaq provides an excellent example during the SMC of 2000 sometimes referred to as the "Millennium Crash" or the "Tech Bubble" since it was driven by an economic decline based on the overvalued technology sector during the young days of the internet at the turn of the millennium. As mentioned before the Nasdaq is a broad market index but it is more concentrated in the technology sector. Just as the XLF chart declined more during the 2008 recession and the BAC chart dropped even more, the technology sector more closely approximated by the Nasdaq index, would suffer more in such a case like the millennium tech bubble.

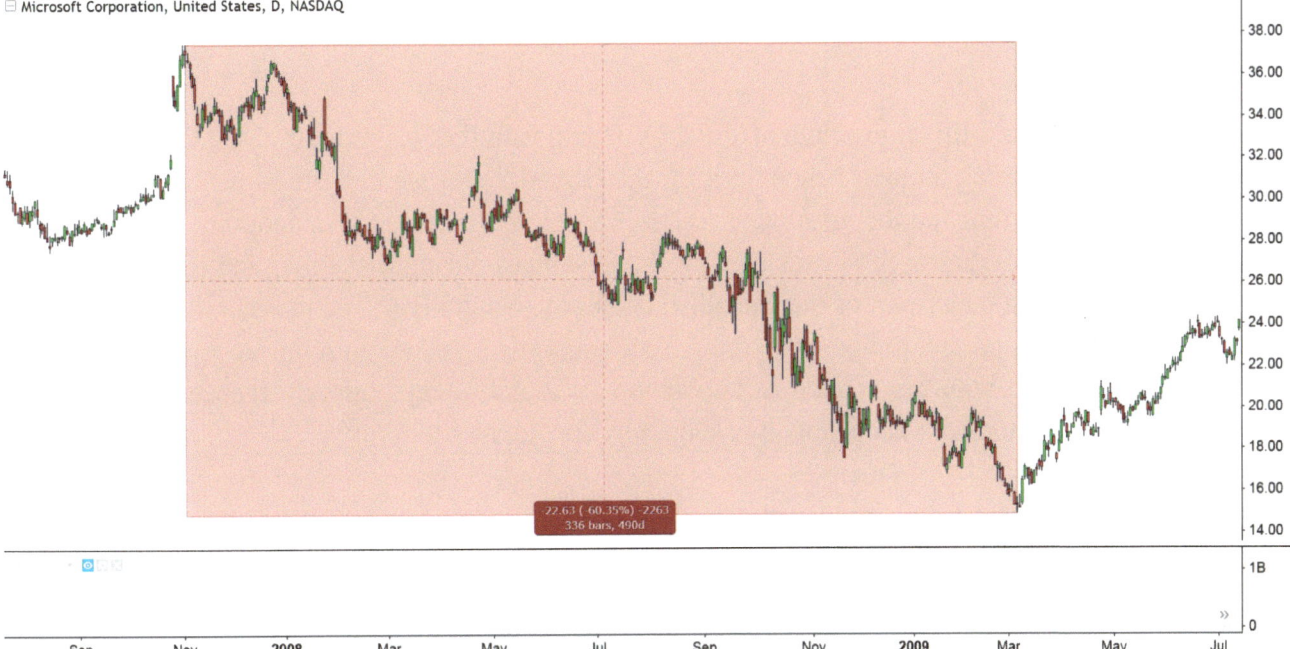

Figure 2.17

Figure 2.18

Since the tech sector was more resilient than the financial sector in the early 21st century it was able to recover from its downturn in 2000 and managed to reduce more severe losses during the 2008 financial sector based decline. Since Microsoft(MSFT) was a major stock within the sector similar to BAC being a major stock in the financial sector, we are presented with a contrasting case. Whereas BAC suffered even more during its sector's decline, MSFT having more favorable conditions survived two SMCs and managed to lessen impacts from both crashes in terms of being an individual stock. In fact since MSFT was a major tech stock but remained relatively strong compared to its peers, particularly those that were more internet based. Microsoft actually dropped slightly less than the overall Nasdaq.

Figure 2.19

Slowly switching gears with an example of the TSX Composite Index, the main Canadian benchmark index. With the Dow being a major benchmark for the United States we can see some variation during the same 2015-2016 time period examined earlier. From a fundamental standpoint the Canadian economy suffered more during the lower demand for resources during that time, and in particular the declining value of oil a major part of the Canadian economy. Naturally the economy effected the stock market. Though it is important to note even though the economy is linked with the stock market and the stock market is linked with the economy. The economy is not always directly representative of the stock market and the stock market is not always directly tied to the economy.

The Stock Market vs. The Economy

The economy can be thought of as the present and past. This goes for most all economic data such as employment figures, spending, debt, and more. The stock market is tied to the happenings of the past and present to an extent. However it is forward facing, investors look for future potential growth and possible risk. Money doesn't go into the stock market solely based on past and present economic conditions. It is a sort of expectation of possible future gains and losses that drives stock markets. Thus economic data and current events can certainly influence the stock market almost immediately, but keep in mind that it is not a direct causal relation. In many cases there is a disparity and/or lag between events up to the present and those of future expectations. That is why stock prices can rise even when the economy presents negative news. In such cases the negative news was not as bad as first expected and/or there is a future expectation for recovery. This in turn creates a disparity between stock market performance and the economy.

The less than direct relation between the stock market and economy can also work the other way during SMCs. Often the immediate mindset in the market in the span of less than a year overestimates future impacts of poor economic performance in the present and past. This often leads to a drastic sell off and over extension downward in a relatively short time compared to slow over inflated expectations when markets become over extended upwards.

As stated before core SMC characteristics from a charting perspective are more useful in that they are more consistent, while fundamental reasons for economic and stock price decline vary from crash to crash. It is more helpful to focus on the metrics discussed from the "Crashometer." It is certainly helpful to understand that the lower demand for oil during the 2015-2016 period negatively impacted the Canadian economy leading to a more sustained drop than the Dow and the American economy during the same time period. Though if we just focus on the simple metrics of a more than 20% drop lasting at least 6 months we can see Canadian markets technically experienced an SMC while American markets only experienced a correction.

One primary reason a 20%-30% drop lasting for at least 6 months is a common minimum threshold range for classifying a drop as an SMC is because that is the approximate metric used for economic data. Economies don't necessarily have to decline in all their key metrics by 20-30% but as long as there is a sustained 6 month period or more of economic contraction where figures decline than a recession is said to occur. This is then related to some degree(but not directly related as discussed above) to the performance of a stock market. Stock markets are often almost directly in sync with economic performance or even slightly ahead in terms of stocks dropping more than would be expected due to poor economic and fundamental performance. Then gradually stock markets soon realize the initial sell off often embodied by a near vertical drop in the span of a few weeks, becomes overblown. Stock markets than move clearly ahead of current and past economic performance and take on a distinctly more optimistic and bullish tone. That is why it is common to hear news expressing doubts and hesitation of an economic recovery when a stock market begins an uptrend reversal because investors and traders lean more to future expectations of growth and further away from initially over exaggerated negativity.

Figure 2.20

The Canadian and American stock indices with the TSX, Dow, and Nasdaq respectively were quite clear in the previous examples. During the compared 2015-2016 time period the TSX clearly crossed the threshold for a minor bear market due to the small recession, while American markets dropped too but remained within the realm of a medium sized correction in a continued long term uptrend. This example in figure 4.0 of Hong Kong's main stock index the Hang Seng, presents a more dynamic case.

At first it is quite similar to what we've seen before with a sustained uptrend that peaks sharply to begin the 2018 new year. This results in a rapid correction which soon finds a temporary range of support. As the first quarter of 2018 ends there is another rapid drop upon break of the temporary support range. At this point the pace of the drop decreases as the 20% barrier is crossed just as the second half of the year begins. Incidentally that designates this to be an SMC based on the minimum criteria which is eventually surpassed as the market continues to plummet until October when it begins a slow but significant reversal.

Eventually a sizable recovery develops to exit the bear market to begin 2019. By no coincidence the recovery is halted around the 30000 area which just so happens to be the major range of temporary support that served as the first pause at the beginning of the SMC. What follows is another sharp drop, minor temporary support range that is broken, leading to another sharp drop, which incidentally forms a strong reversal in October around the same 25000 area.

Thus we see the same basic core features. A long term uptrend is reversed either sharply or more gradually, in this case sharply. The start of the SMC is a rapid drop that crosses the 10% criteria to become a medium sized correction over the span of a few weeks. A temporary but significant short term support range forms. It is at this point the market hinges on an SMC. Once the temporary support range is broken it leads to another sharp drop which gradually begins to slow down, and with time leads to a recovery of significant proportions.

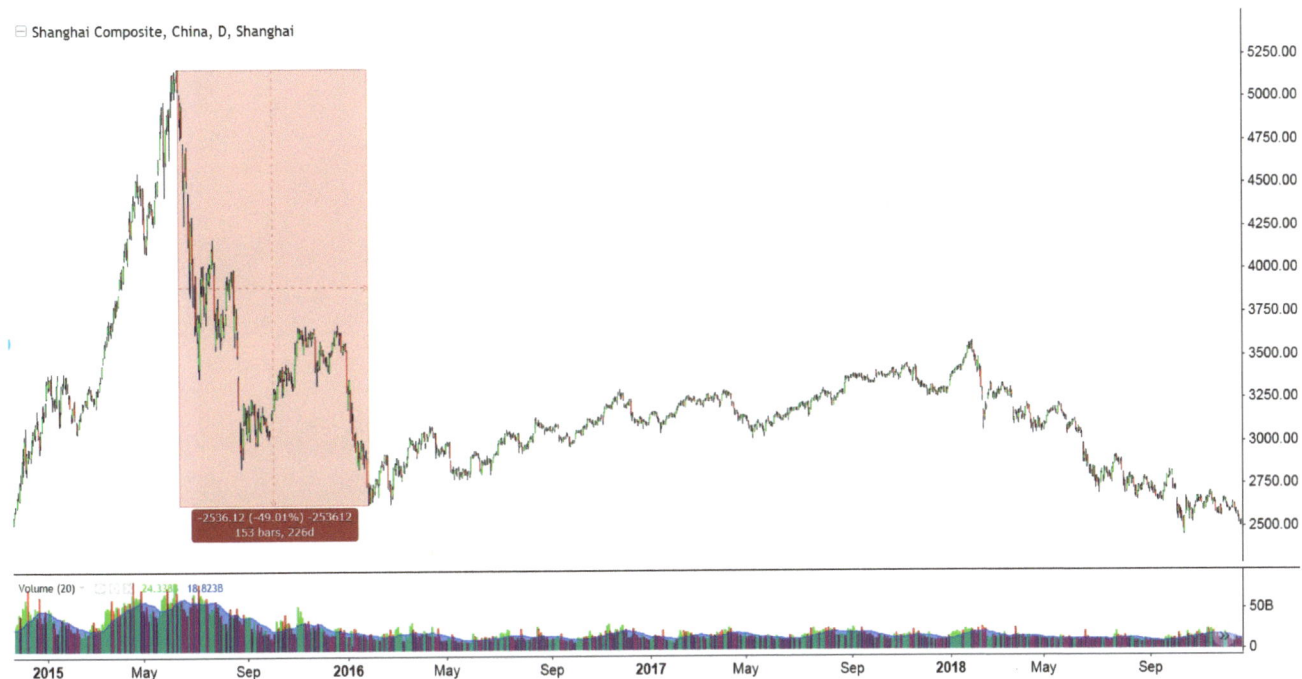

Figure 2.21

Like the Hang Seng example the Shanghai Composite Index undergoes an SMC and develops a major upward reversal. In this case to begin 2016 on an uptrend around the 2500 area. The uptrend continues for over a year but eventually finds strong resistance at the intermediate area that formed the initial temporary supporting range and later resistance around the high 3000s to low 4000s range. Like the Hang Seng chart it leads to a major reversal back to the lows which are passed in this case as the market heads even lower.

As was discussed earlier there is debate over what constitutes an SMC and there will never be complete agreement. However as we have seen the common minimum criteria of a 20% drop lasting at least 6 months is a useful guideline. What is even more debatable is defining the criteria to designate a market as recovered and no longer in an SMC. The first few cases of the Dow, Nasdaq, and TSX were quite straightforward. In most cases the market simply reversed back up to eventually pass the high where the SMC began, often to reach new record high ranges.

Figure 2.22

The examples of the Hong Kong and Shanghai indices are somewhat more difficult to determine. They technically did form upward reversals to end their respective SMCs. On the other hand the so called recoveries only produced up trends that regained a portion of the lost value from the SMCs. Moreover these up trends were short lived and these stock markets went back to retest their SMC lows. For the Hang Seng this meant a large intermediate range formed from the mid 20000s to low 30000s. Eventually the original lows around 25000 were broken and like with the breaking of most all major supporting ranges there was a rapid free fall before the market began to stabilize and recover slightly. Even when the newest up trend formed it was slow as usual in comparison to the rapid drop prior and it experienced heavy resistance at a prior major support range that previously paused the long term market descent.

It could be argued that the Hong Kong stock market had recovered to some degree or even that the SMC was over during the final quarter of 2019 during the first major upward reversal. However that would soon be debatable when early 2020 saw the market fall back to the original lows. At that point the most optimistic assessment could still say the market was not recovered but the SMC was over with the market in a neutral phase. That would be a stretch but there would be some rationale for that argument during that first quarter of 2020 when the mid 20000s continued to hold even during a renewed spike down. Though once the support range was eventually passed well below 25000 even the most optimistic assessments could not deny the fact the longer term downtrend had resumed and that the short to medium term was very much bearish. Additionally it is no surprise the most recent recovery shown on the chart found major resistance at the last significant supporting range around the 25000 area.

Figure 2.23

The case of the Shanghai Composite is an even more extreme example of a market that has not recovered. The Hang Seng chart was at least able to regain 50% or more of the lost value at some points of the SMC for a sustained time span. However the Shanghai Composite did not manage to do so. It is sometimes reasoned a market can be partially recovered and out of an SMC in a slightly bearish to neutral phase in the long term if it has at least regained 50% of the initial lost value from high to low of the SMC range such as in the case of the Hang Seng during its first upward reversals.

No such bullish initiative in the Shanghai market and after mid 2018 saw even lower lows the resumption of the long term downtrend was in full force once again. Subsequent upward reversals were large into 2019 and 2020 but they never reached anywhere near a 50% recovery of lost value from the initial 2015 SMC highs to the early 2016 lows that began the first decent up trend that later failed.

The use of Fibonacci Retracements is an excellent way to easily see if a market has at least partially recovered and potentially ended an SMC. Simply take the high and extend to the low as shown in Figure 2.23 and see if the uptrend starting from the low has reached the .5 level which is 50% of the SMC range. SMCs are truly just large scale price drops/corrections. The Fibonacci Retracement can be applied to other examples that displayed major support/resistance zones. The same basic technical analysis principles are seen regarding price action and its behavior around contentious areas. The only difference is the larger magnitude with the price ranges and the longer term impact that can be seen over the span of months, years, and even decades. Thus it is very helpful to understand basic yet effective technical analysis with trends, support, and resistance. As well as building to more intermediate to advanced methods such as chart patterns and Fibonacci Retracements which as seen are very useful in determining when a chart crosses a temporary range to go from medium correction to full scale SMC. A solid base of technical analysis skill to analyze charts can compliment fundamental analysis which will be discussed to some degree later. Such charting skills also lend well to "rare and unusual events," "freak events" or even "black swan events" which are rare and/or unforeseen events that rock the market in a similar way to SMCs.

Figure 2.24

The Brexit vote in June 2016 provides an excellent example of this category of events. It was foreseen but it was a relatively rare kind of event, even historic some would say in terms of the market impact. Lots of uncertainty and negative sentiment culminated in a volatile but short lived drop. By the roughly 8.67% drop it is a small drop but due to the rapid pace it resembles the speed seen in large corrections or SMCs.

Figure 2.25

Thus while such a drop due to the uncertainty of a planned and expected event like Brexit was very bearish in the short term it had a low impact in terms of market price action in the grand scheme of things when referring to that one week during the Brexit vote. Some may call such events "micro crashes" or "mini crashes" because they are small in terms of the scale of the price drop, but the volatility and associated panic are similar to that found in SMCs.

Overall the markets in Britain, Europe, and around the world were effected but soon recovered quickly due to the planned nature of this event. Every one knew it was coming for a long time and there was a scheduled date for the Brexit vote. No great magnitude was reached here because the temporary uncertainty was over quite quickly and everything else was not unforeseen or "out of the blue "so to speak. Regardless of whether people liked the outcome of Brexit politically or in other aspects the end result from a charting standpoint saw a scheduled event of high uncertainty pass rapidly.

Figure 2.26

Unlike Brexit the September 11th attacks in 2001 were on the opposite end of the spectrum in that they were largely unforeseen by the broad masses and the stock market was no exception. Of course with the benefit of hindsight on a historic level "9/11" had some warning signs given the context of events from the late 70s to late 90s in the middle east however it would not have been reasonable for traders and investors, let alone the general public to declare such an event would take place exactly the way it did.

In any case the objective here is mainly focused on the chart and not so much the underlying event(s). Due to the contrasting unpredictable and unexpected nature of "9/11" the immediate drop during that week was larger and slightly longer lasting than what was seen with Brexit.

Figure 2.27

Furthermore in the bigger picture the effects lasted longer as a longer term downtrend resumed. Figure 2.26 and Figure 2.27 use the SPY ETF which tracks the S&P 500 index. It is also a broad market representation like the classic Dow and the Nasdaq seen earlier. It has some variation but is still an overall representation of the American stock market. If you recall during the early 2000s the stock markets were still under the influence of the "tech bubble" crash and "9/11" only worsened the longer term situation.

However in the short term as better illustrated by figure 2.26 "9/11" like Brexit was on a downward over extension in stock prices due to short term fear and uncertainty.

Flash Crashes

Flash Crashes are perhaps the scariest of events because of their mysterious nature. Events like Brexit are scheduled so they have less fear surrounding them. Cases like "9/11" are scarier due to the largely unforeseeable nature of such events. However there is still some "comfort" in that a relatively straightforward connection exists between a terrorist attack and declining stock prices due to fear and uncertainty. Moreover even if a clear connection was less apparent between an unforeseen event and falling stock prices, the context of a chart being in a long term downtrend like in the early 2000s at least gives a partial explanation from a technical analysis perspective.

Flash Crashes discard everything because they happen suddenly, are virtually unpredictable, and it is often difficult to explain fully why or how they developed to a satisfactory degree.

Figure 2.28

The term "Flash Crash" had been around for decades and likely originates from a comparison to flash floods. The term only reached the forefront of widespread public attention during the famous "2010 Flash Crash." After this crash the term became more well known and was first commonly associated with the 2010 event. At the time it was completely unpredictable such an event would take place. Panic selling was allegedly initiated by a significant enough amount of sell orders of "e-minis" futures contracts that track the S&P500 index. This is one of the most popular theories explaining the crash but is still only said to be one of a number of factors that contributed to the rapid sell off. To make things even more amazing is the claim that an individual trader located in London was the one who started the panic selling.

The flash crash of 2010 may never be fully explained with 100% certainty but it does serve to highlight the vulnerability of modern stock exchanges which can experience technical difficulties along with intentional and unintentional manipulation that can trigger immediate sell offs that seemingly appear out of nowhere. As a consequence some measures are in place to defend or more accurately mitigate such events. For example some stock exchanges may shut down and halt all trading during a detected technical difficulty or after a rapid price drop has occurred in less than a day and some manipulation or technical failure is suspected. Some speculation surrounds the decline of the Shanghai Index seen in figures 2.21 and 2.23, because it has been stated part of the decline can be attributed to a series of flash crashes that developed from panic selling that was started by irregular amounts of short selling. Additionally the situation was possibly worsened by supposed technical difficulties with the Shanghai stock exchange in the proceeding years combined with the underlying slow down of the Chinese economy and related lower enthusiasm of investors.

Then going back to the chart in figure 2.28 it can be reasoned that if the flash crash didn't occur the market may not have continued the minor downward reversal from April much further or longer. Though that is only speculation and hypothetical reasoning. Perhaps the market still would have dropped but at a far slower pace and with lower volatility. As you may notice there is much more speculative and conditional language used when discussing flash crashes. Such language is mainly used because of the lack of certainty in adequately explaining these mysterious events.

Figure 2.29

(Monthly chart of the Dow Jones Industrial Average)

The crash referred to simply as the "1987" crash has sometimes been called a flash crash because it meets all the criteria of a more than 20% drop for a traditional SMC but not lasting the minimum 6 months. However it does have characteristics of a flash crash and sudden drops(like "9/11" and Brexit) because of the rapid pace the market fell at during such a short time span. Additionally like a flash crash a satisfactory explanation has yet to fully explain the cause(s) of this SMC with any great certainty. In fact it is sometimes reasoned the stock market simply needed a correction and it eventually did happen, which would explain why in the long term we see a very healthy up trend develop into the 1990s to continue on the healthy trajectory seen prior, especially around the second half of 1986.

Nonetheless we still see core SMC features in these past 4 examples of exceptional cases. A downswing begins to form or there is already a preexisting downtrend before these sudden events. Then as usual the market surges down except at an even more accelerated pace. If the events are short lived like Brexit the market pulls back up after a very brief support range has formed. In other cases like the 2010 flash crash or 9/11, and even the 1987 crash the market pauses briefly as seen with the traditional SMCs before breaking the temporary support range that acts as a critical threshold separating a small to medium sized correction from becoming an SMC. Though of course with the 9/11 and 2010 flash crash examples these are seen on a much smaller scale but at a more rapid pace. Finally the process continues with the second bearish spike gradually slowing down to form a volatile upswing that soon settles down into a slow up trend.

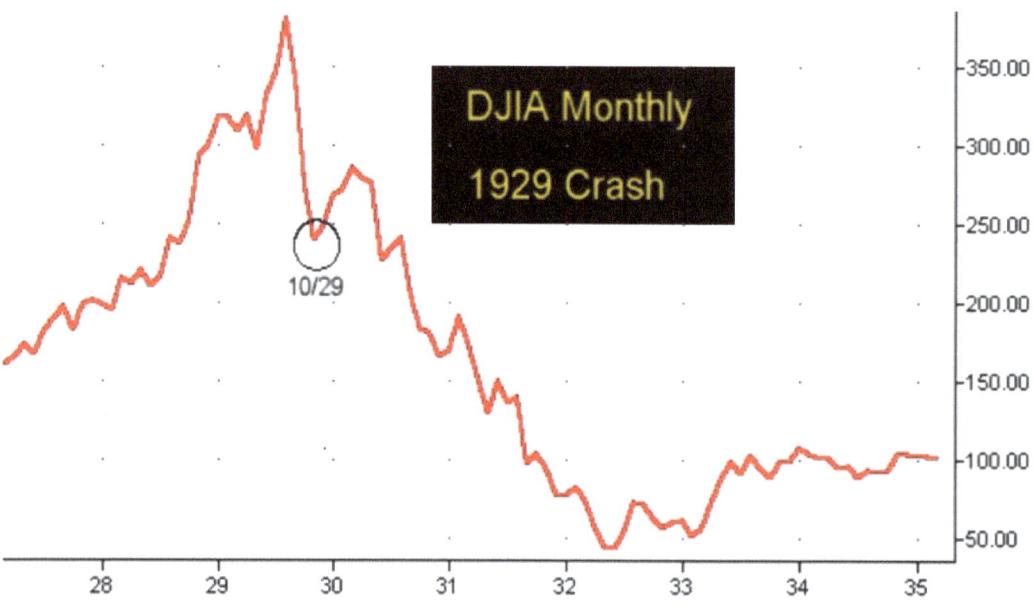

Figure 2.30

(Monthly line chart of the Dow Jones Industrial Average)

Lastly we see the "grandfather" of modern SMCs in figure 2.30 during the historic 1929 SMC. Once again we see the same characteristics the have become an overarching theme in the story of SMCs. A long term uptrend ends in 1929 to bring the "roaring 20s" to an end. To make things worse this is a sharp peak as the market undertook a steep climb before reaching its high. This led to the rubber band effect with an equally steep move down to begin the first portion of the crash that pauses with a temporary support range that formed around October 29th. Then once this short term range is broken it triggers the classic free fall after an influential support is passed. There is a gradual slow down before the market eventually bottomed out.

It can be said the run up to a crash has no defined time or price range only that the market is on an uptrend for an extended time, often for years. Then it peaks either gradually or sharply, this usually takes several weeks to two months as we have seen. When the downtrend is fully underway with the first rapid spike to the minor supporting range the time and price range varies. However usually it will be less than a 20% decline which often leads to ambiguity in the short term of whether it is a correction or a young SMC in development. The important thing to note is that the temporary supporting range is the critical border and can often be identified by using basic swing points to plot a support range, or you can use chart patterns and Fibonacci Retracements if applicable. This temporary supporting range also varies in duration but usually lasts for less than a year often less than 8 months. Additionally this first phase from market peak to temporary support range usually measures roughly 1/5 to 2/5 of the entire length of an SMCs price and time range. That is why it often forms around the first two Fibonacci levels.

Then the next phase normally sees the emergence of an SMC when the 20% price drop threshold is surpassed after a break of the temporary support. This again happens at a relatively more rapid pace before gradually slowing down. Normally the SMC is ½ to 2/3 complete in price and time range. If it is a prolonged SMC like the 1929 crash or the Shanghai Composite Index of the mid 2010s-2020s the steps may continue again, or the market flattens out but doesn't recover similar to what was seen with the Hang Seng chart.

Finally it can be said the crash is over when an uptrend forms and there is no breech of this defined low where the up trend began. After that the market moves on to partial recovery if it regains at least 50% of its lost value from peak to recently established bottom at the upswing of the current uptrend that must make clear higher highs and higher lows. Next a market is only fully recovered from an SMC once it surpasses the high where the crash began and continues upward.

By understanding the approximate thresholds that separate the dynamic phases of SMCs, investors and traders can better recognize situations where extended bull markets present risk of a medium correction evolving into an SMC. Better determinations can also be made to exit the market and get ready to reenter at a later time once a temporary support range has been identified following a rapid drop from a potential peak. Such temporary support ranges are key areas that appeared in example after example, once they were breached markets entered SMC territory.

Additional benefits can be gained by identifying lower supporting ranges after the market resumes another sharp drop. In doing so more losses can be avoided and chances of reentering the market at even lower prices are increased. Also it is helpful to understand partial and full recoveries in order to determine the health of a market after an SMC stops making lower lows.

Chapter 3

Causes And Contributing Factors In Stock Market Crashes

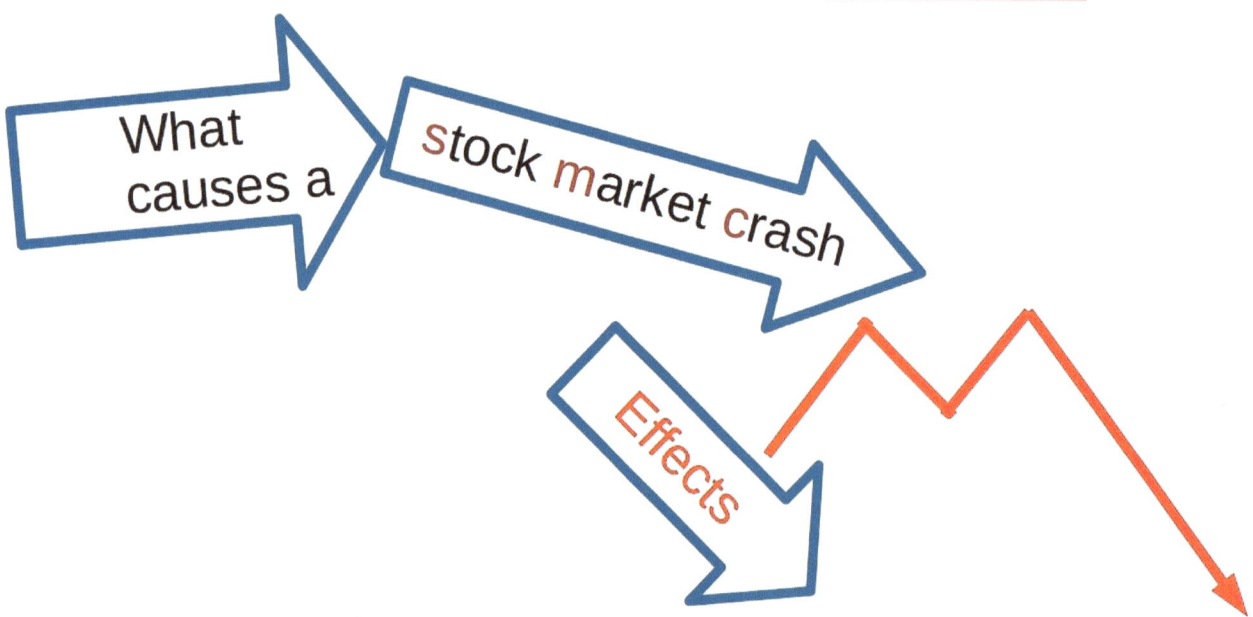

Figure 3.0

It is often more realistic to explain an SMC with fundamental factors by using a combination of contributing factors since stock markets like all financial markets are driven by dynamic factors, rather than a rigid set of predefined criteria. That is why we will slowly transition from the core SMC characteristics conveniently summarized in the structure of price action seen on charts, to the incorporation of fundamental factors behind major market moves.

So what causes an SMC? Like any good answer "it depends" no two crashes are exactly the same, unique combinations of fundamental factors underlie the consistently similar characteristics of stock charts falling in value. In the following series of diagrams the most common fundamental factors behind SMCs will be highlighted. This enhances understanding of SMCs but is not completely necessary. It is only a compliment to the consistently objective metrics seen on charts. Fundamental factors can be objective but carry a degree of subjectivity especially when an event related to an SMC can't readily be quantified, we shall see several examples of that shortly.

Figure 3.1

A simple answer to a complex and varying question is SMCs are caused by inflated expectations. This normally refers to over optimism that drives the characteristics of bullish trends prior to a chart peaking and crashing. This is in part why analogies like "hot air" and "bubble bursting" are used when talking about SMCs. Like balloons, bubbles, and hot air the markets are inflated up and eventually pop either due to an explosion, which is reflected on charts as over extension and sharp peaking. As well it can also be largely due to just a pin popping an otherwise healthy market that is not inflated. This is reflected more so when an uptrend is not necessarily inflated, it may actually not be over extended upward. However the proverbial bubble bursts due to unforeseen events such as those discussed in chapter 2, especially regarding flash crashes with no clear explanation. This relates to over inflated expectations secondarily referring to over blown fear in the markets. A healthy market can collapse due to an injection of over exaggerated fear following an unforeseen event that rapidly reduces stock prices. Furthermore an over inflated market can collapse even more spectacularly due to sudden and unforeseen events like 9/11 which extended the bear market originating from the popping of the tech bubble.

Figure 3.2

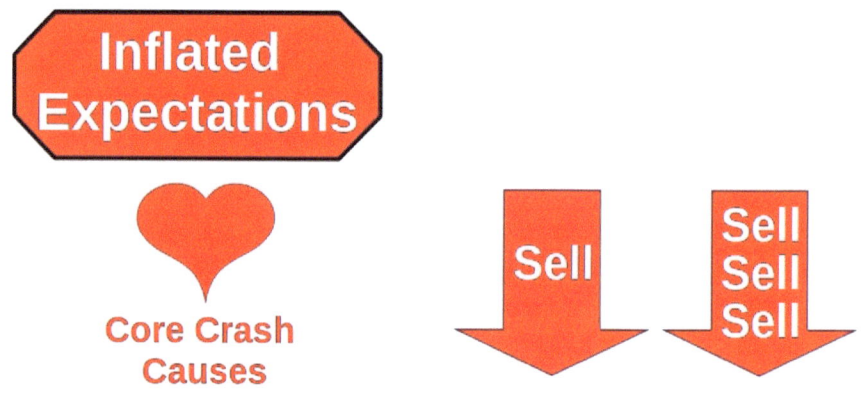

Figure 3.3

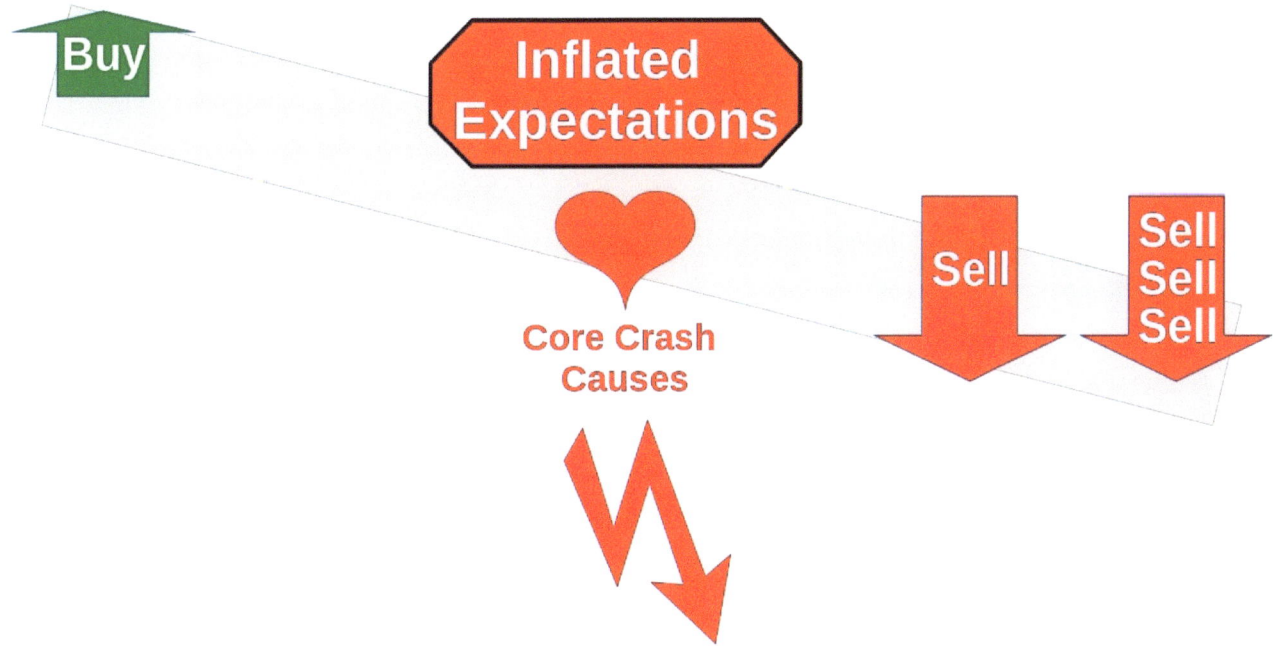

Figure 3.4

Figures 3.2 to 3.4 illustrate the classic SMC phenomenon where a market has risen too high and begins to correct and eventually reverse into a heavy sell off. The millennium crash with the tech bubble and the 2008 recession are classic examples, along with the historic case of the 1929 crash. Those three crashes had differing combinations of fundamental factors but they all revolve around the central idea of over inflated expectations that can't be sustained, which leads to a crash that first peaks and corrects. Then after that first phase where the temporary support is broken, the majority of the crash is triggered and markets plunge much lower.

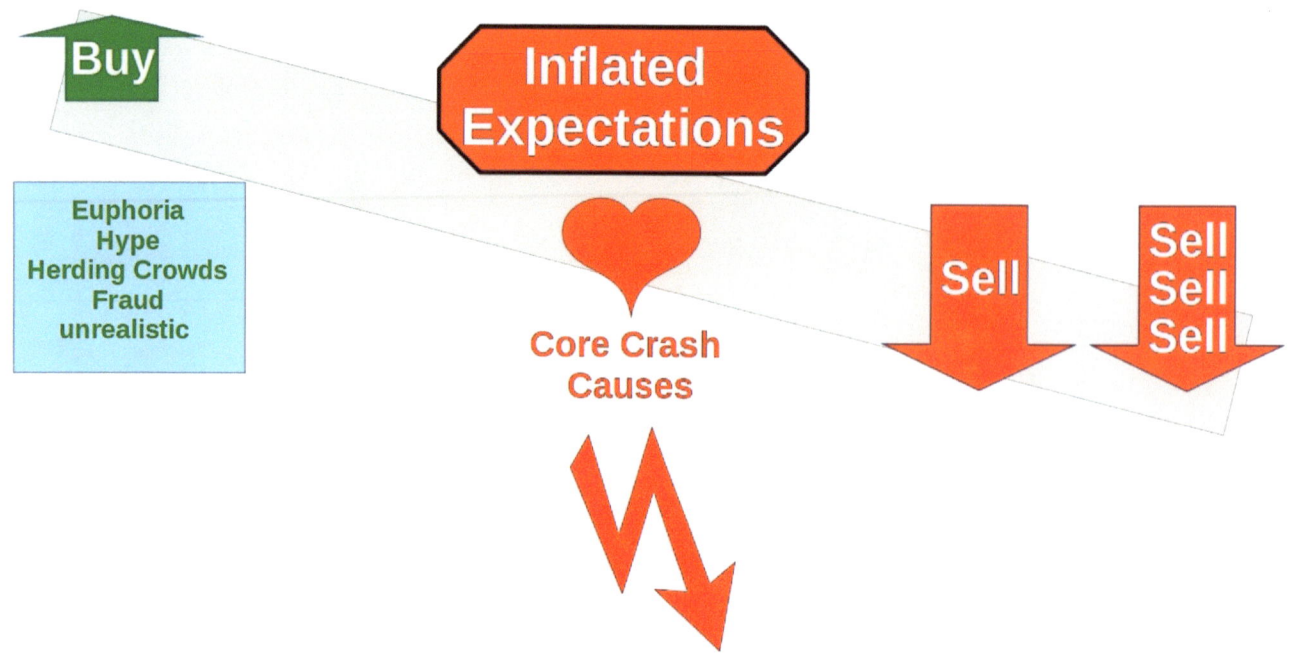

Figure 3.5

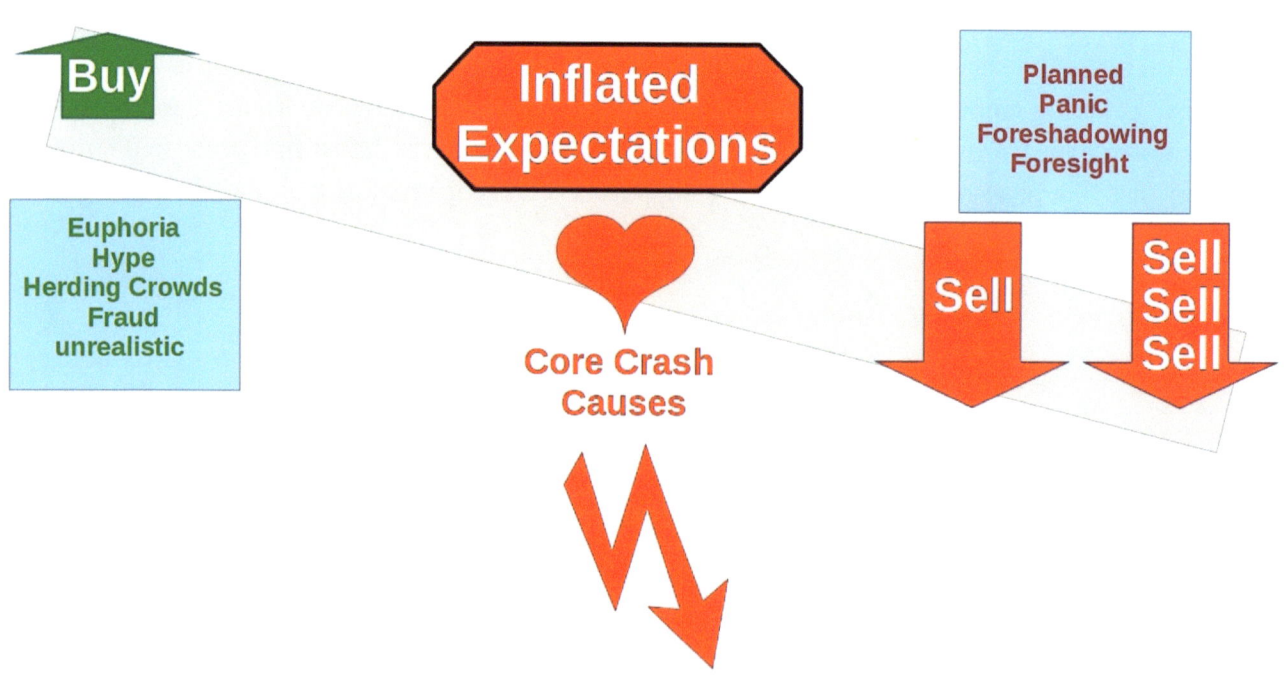

Figure 3.6

Figures 3.5 and 3.6 elaborate further with broad categories of influences that tip market balance from a buyer's market to a seller's market. On the buy side there are the classic forces of euphoria and hype. Again each crash is different but essentially the buy side gets to an over extended point due to exaggerated expectations driving on for too long. Eventually buying will be exhausted and tip in favor of a sellers market. The phenomenon can be natural unrealistic expectations and/or intentional fraudulent manipulation. For example inflated expectations behind the internet with the tech bubble in 2000 and the financing of real estate leading up to the 2008 SMC were certainly driven by genuine crowd behavior. Initial bullish sentiment was renewed again and again as more buyers joined in. However there were indeed manipulative and fraudulent forces at work behind these cases, which only served to worsen the situation once it became apparent the markets were grossly overvalued and overbought at those times for the reasoning given.

That is why it is quite appropriate to say the tipping of market favor to the sell side in those or any other SMC case was a "planned panic." Such a term is used because the stock market or simply "the market(s)" can be thought of as an entity made up of individual traders and investors. They can be single individuals as well as institutions. The point is the market is a collective mass and like any crowd it is driven by a myriad of dynamic factors. However at the end of the day there will usually be a few predominating factors that drive the behavior of most of the market participants whether they be short term traders, long term investors, or small individuals and large institutions.

Regardless of the exact causes of each SMC the herd that is the stock market will be led towards the path of panic selling that progressively increases and pauses at certain points. As seen in chapter two the first key point that is summarized on a chart is when the market fails to regain a recent high it has made. After that there is the distinct first spike down until the first range of temporary support that was seen in example after example. The breaking of that first temporary support is what accelerates the SMC into full gear after the initial drop from the peak and downward reversal. Panic seems completely random but whether there is manipulation or it is a fully natural crash the market always panics to a greater degree after the first temporary support range is broken. Thus each SMC is largely predetermined in the way the market will behave at key thresholds. Reasoning for selling will be different for each trader and investor in each market during each SMC. However there is a degree of foresight in terms of how the market will fall once key supporting ranges are identified.

The increased use of artificial intelligence to trade and invest based on algorithms is said to be more rational and stable for the markets since machines won't be emotional like a crowd of humans. However it must be remembered humans are still the ones programming the models and even if artificial intelligence becomes fully autonomous algorithms are not infallible and/or immune to broader market forces. In fact algorithmic based trading and investing done by computers can worsen and accelerate panic selling in situations such as flash crashes due to the near instantaneous execution of sell orders by machines.

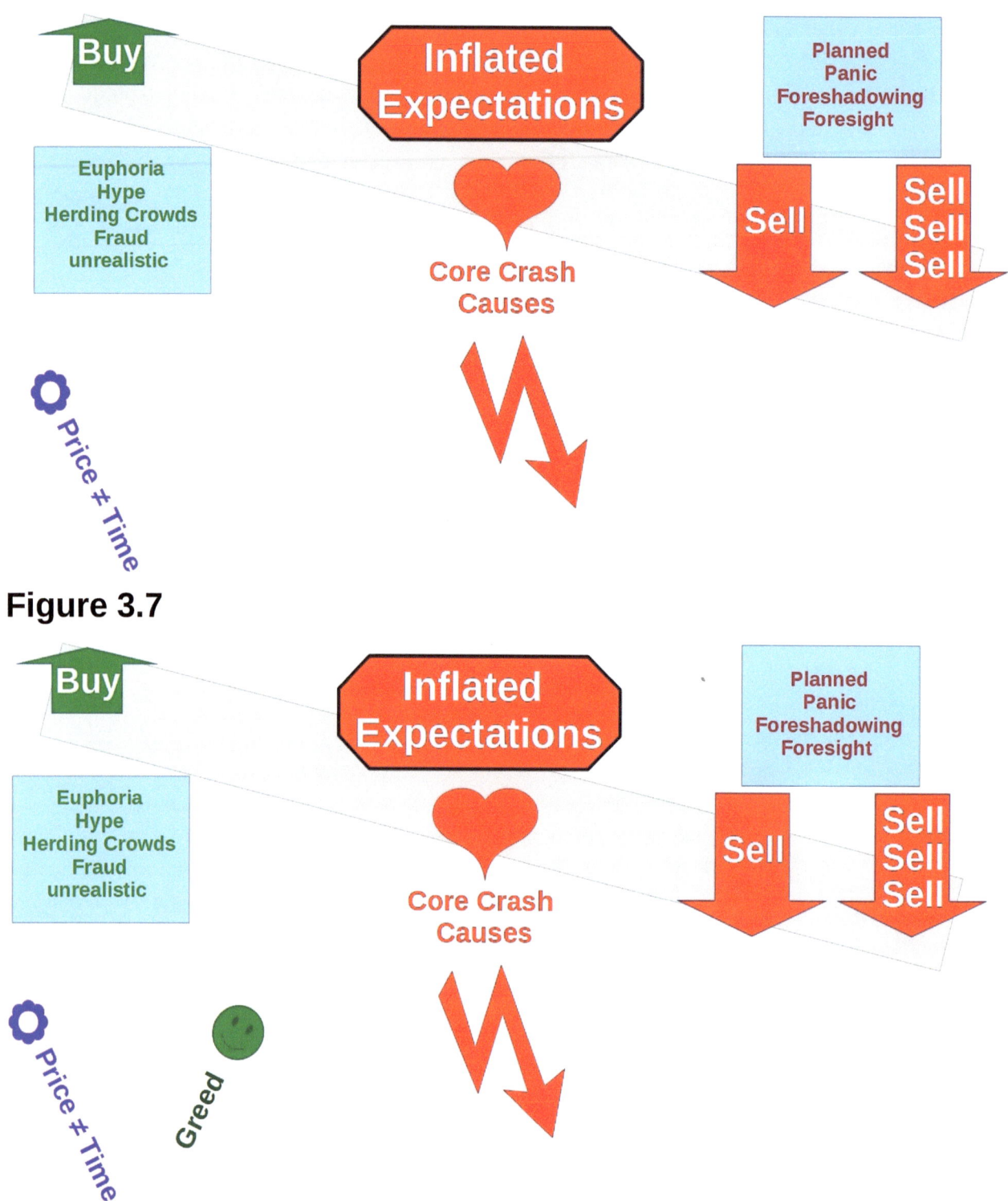

Figure 3.7

Figure 3.8

An SMC cannot be perfectly timed that is why there is no exact rule or ratio as to how much stock prices can rise and for how long before a crash must happen. Though it is useful to keep in mind the approximate metrics discussed in chapters one and two to determine how far over extended a market is in order to gauge the increased chances of a crash if no small or moderate corrections occur for an extended period of time. Greed has no limits the market can keep rising based on any combination of unreasonable valuations, it doesn't have to stop because price has risen a certain amount or duration. It is only more likely the market will at least correct once it begins to become over extended during a prolonged uptrend.

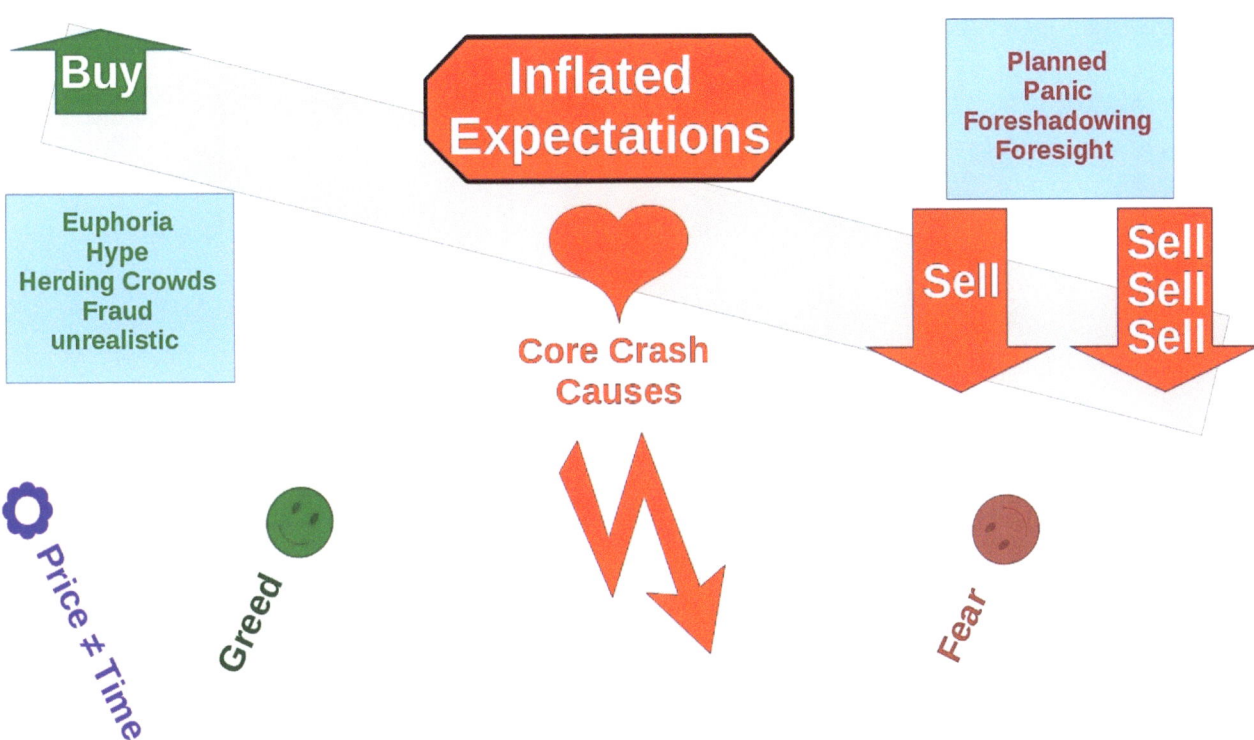

Figure 3.9

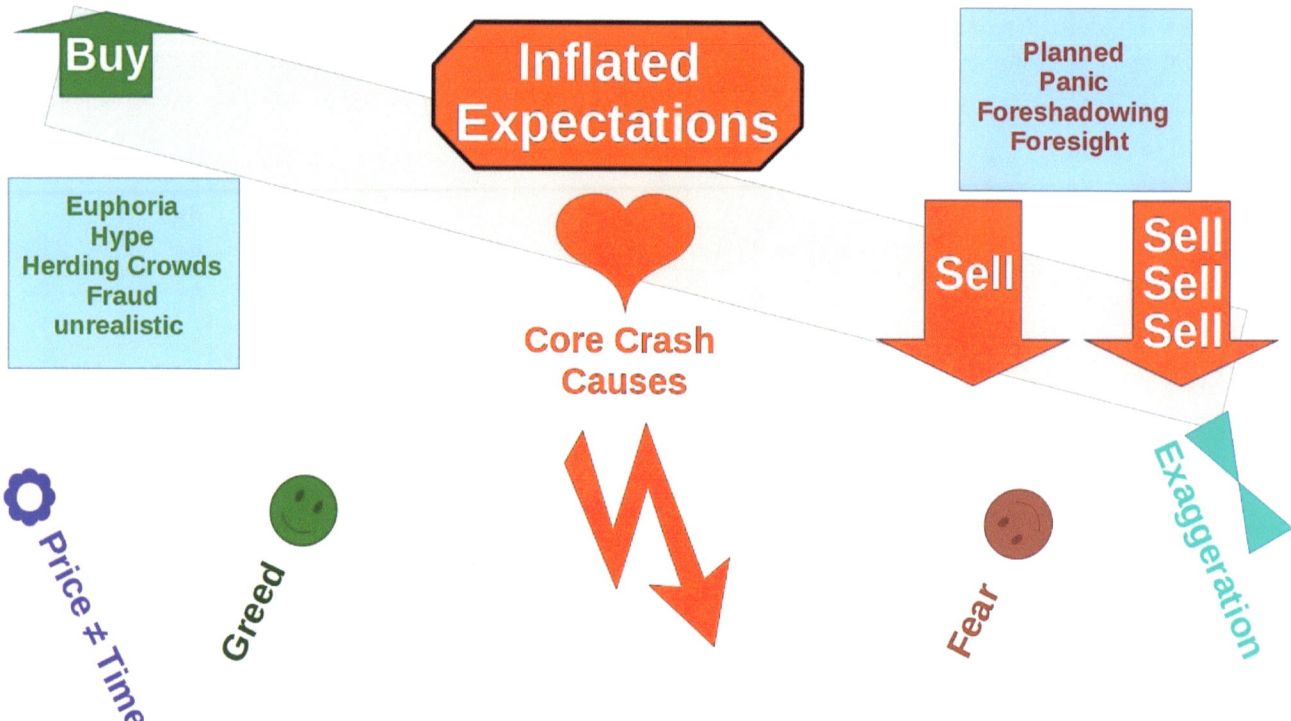

Figure 3.10

On the sell side it is also true that fear knows no exaggeration. It is easy to look back with a calm mindset at SMCs of the past and think about how you would act so much more rationally. However that is only with the benefit of hindsight and free of the circumstance and pressure that exists during the midst of an SMC in progress. That is why the first bought of selling is often not the most impactful part of an SMC. Rather it is the accelerated panic selling that occurs after the first temporary support range is broken. Thereby taking a normal correction towards SMC territory. The first bought of selling may actually be quite natural in correcting the market. However once panic sets in market participants behave like a herd trying to find the nearest exit. Fear soon becomes practically the only rationale for selling and that creates an effect of the market selling off further and faster.

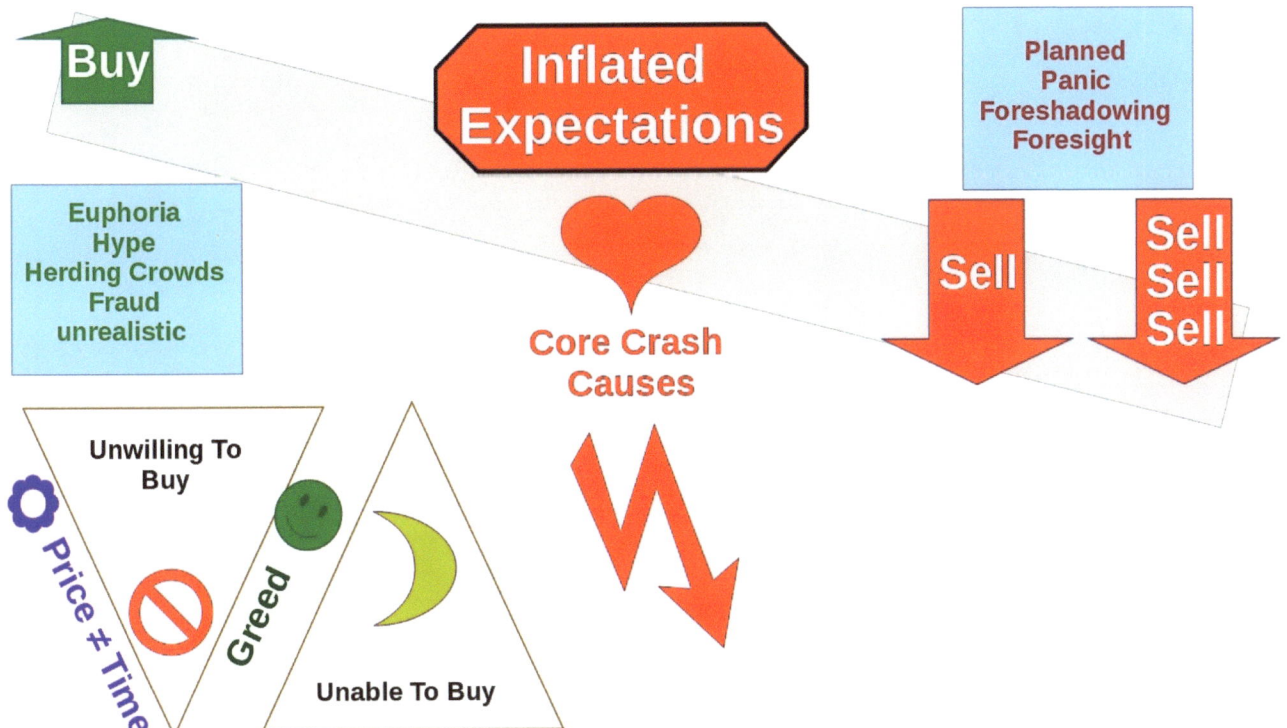

Figure 3.11

The disparity between expectation and reality leads to a multifaceted downfall that underpins every SMC. A rational correction can set about an unwillingness to buy into the market further. Since market participants have become so accustomed to newer high after newer high even a 5-15% correction halting newer highs for a short time can cause anxiety. On the other hand buyers might also be unable to buy especially in cases when the market has largely been propped up through borrowed money which virtually always results in an extra hard crash due to the added dimension of margin and debt.

The combination of the inability and unwillingness to buy are the two primary forces that pause an uptrend and ultimately lead to the birth of a downward reversal that then evolves into a small or medium correction, and later an SMC.

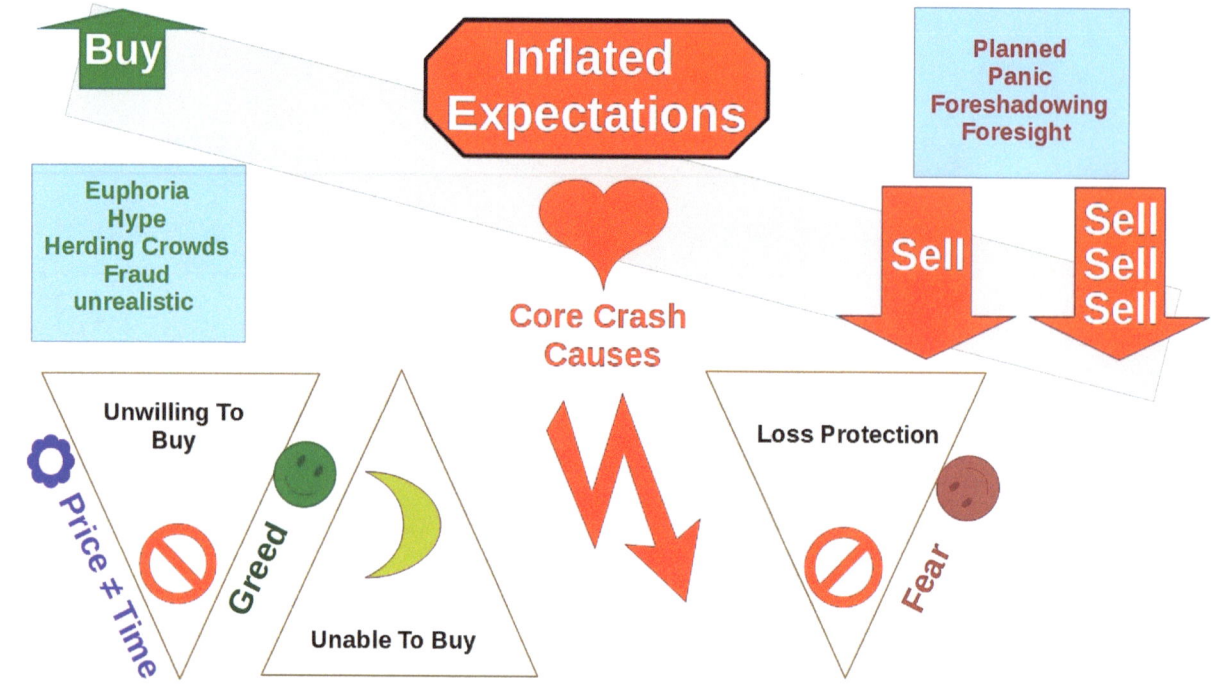

Figure 3.12

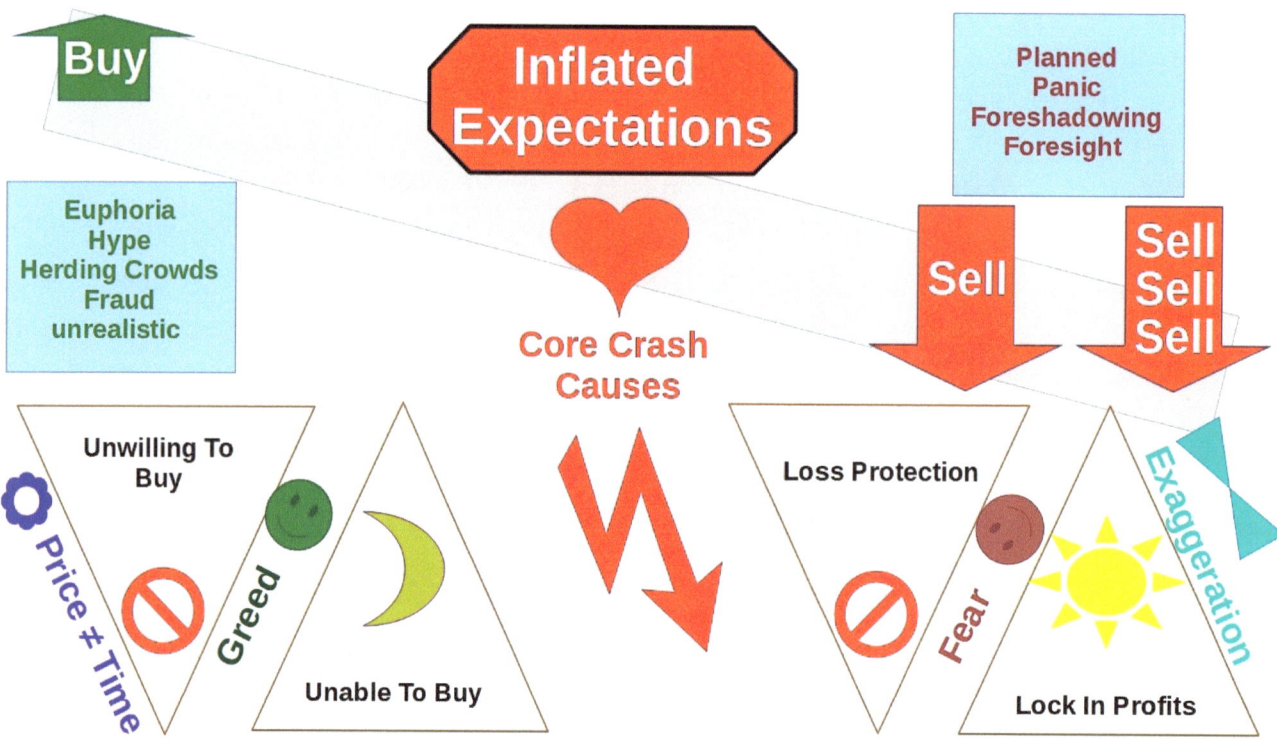

Figure 3.13

On the sell side exaggerated fear is only compounded by the instinct of self preservation. Market participants begin to fall into that naturally predetermined plan for the herd by the time the first bought of selling pauses and develops the first temporary support range. At this point market participants are waiting to see if the small or medium correction breaks through the brief support range to initiate a further drop heading towards a full SMC. If the market later drops into an SMC there will be traders and investors who have already prepared and/or anticipated such a move for a long time and have already planned to begin selling their holding before or shortly after the key threshold is breached. This key threshold is of course the first temporary supporting range. Then there is the rest of the market that will either continue to hold on or begin hasty preparations to sell off their holdings in order to also try and avoid further losses. In any case this point is a critical point during the first portion of an SMC where there is a major shift from buying into the market towards looking for a close and fast exit that will avoid or reduce impending losses. As well as capture and secure as much profits as possible that have yet to be realized from the preceding uptrend that has recently begun to reverse.

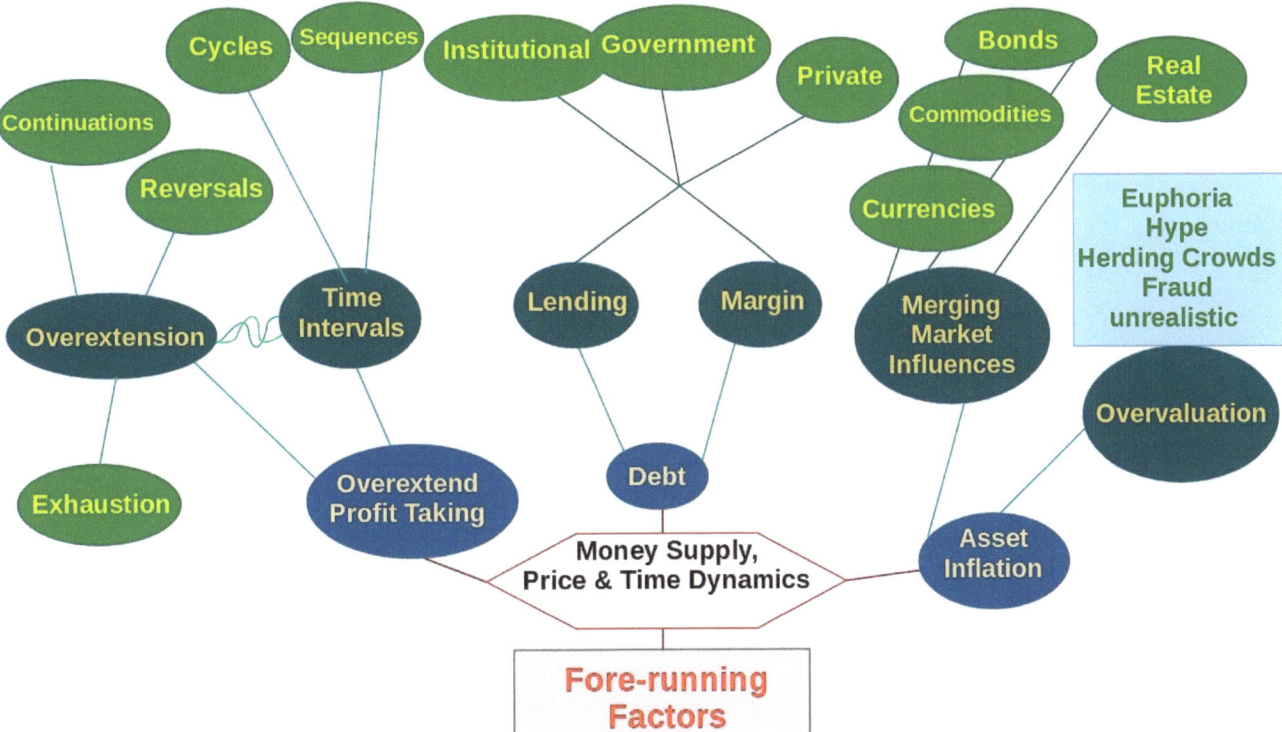

Figure 3.14

Figure 3.14 outlines the main categories and subcategories that can be classified as "Fore-running Factors," which are circumstances that can be predicted to some degree as likely to contribute to an SMC. They all relate to the premise of money supply that is so often linked to SMCs. In particular the idea of stock prices being inflated due to an overabundance of easily lent money that inflates a stock market for seemingly indefinite periods of time.

The middle branch is quite straightforward, think the 1929 and 2008 SMCs as prime examples where irresponsible money lending allowed for stocks to be bought on margin for an extended time, eventually leading to a full scale SMC that involved institutions like banks, government organizations, along with private lending.

The branch on the right side concerns asset inflation that doesn't necessarily just have to be the direct inflation of stock prices. It can concern overvaluation of other markets such as currencies, commodities, bonds, and real estate. This naturally merges the combined influence of multiple markets that will contribute to an SMC. The 2008 recession remains a classic example of overvalued real estate contributing to an SMC. As well the intertwined nature of currencies and commodities impacting stock markets can really be seen with stock markets that are in regions where economies are heavily dependent on resources. Thus the normal fluctuations in commodity prices and currency exchange rates can often have a role in SMCs. For instance the example of the small Canadian SMC seen with the TSX chart in figure 2.19 during a time when the resource reliant Canadian economy slumped more due to lower demand for energy and metals at the time.

Although it is not directly related to SMCs the so called "Crypto Crash" of Bitcoin and cryptocurrencies in general during late 2017-2018 provides another example of asset inflation driven by a market propped up in part buy investing on margin. Furthermore Bitcoin and the cryptocurrency market as a whole were over extended and inflated during that particular time when the primal forces of hype and euphoria were at work. Especially during the time when cryptocurrencies entered the forefront of general public attention which also led to a degree of unrealistic and even fraudulent activity with lesser known cryptocurrencies.

The branch on the left side covers the technical side of trading and investing with charting and also deals with the more farsighted type of investor. This mainly refers to those investors who are able and willing to begin taking profits since they have the skill and ability to recognize the looming consequences of asset inflation driven by investing on margin. Indeed such market participants with this rare combination of willingness and skill are rare. This is largely because it is less common for technical analysis of charts and fundamental analysis of macro factors to be blended in an effective manner, often due to a lack of skill and/or readiness to except the realities of combining multiple types of analysis. Then even if such an individual or institution has the skill there needs to be the willingness to act in a rationale manner in order to lock in profits and reduce losses. In a way such advanced profit taking due to the realization the market is overextended can inadvertently speed up the onset of an SMC due to a seemingly unwarranted spike in selling in the eyes of the broad masses that are more ignorant of the overextended reality. It may even appear as though such an uptick in selling resembles a flash crash, which can lead to panic.

Figure 3.15

Figure 3.15 outlines the main categories and subcategories that can be classified as "Pending Uncertainty" factors. They are similar to those from figure 3.14 in that they are predictable and the extent of their impact can be measured to some degree in advance of a potential SMC. They are essentially the variables that can be known to some extent.

Starting from the right side with a broad macro view there are the factors of slow, low, or even no growth that are often intrinsically related to the peak of a market. In many cases where the market peaks in a slower fashion with several small reversals as opposed to one sharp top, the main factors behind this are stagnation and later contraction of the macro economy. The 2008 recession is a good example of this as such slow down was largely foreseen and constantly talked about, which is why the decline seen in 2008 was less steep of a drop. Instead there were charts that more slowly and gradually slid in value in comparison to other more rapid SMCs. As crashes like the 2008 recession progress they are still at a relatively moderate pace on the way down with some occasional surges. However the overall tone is of hesitation, and low or no confidence. While there is uncertainty it is not to the same degree as SMCs that are driven by factors that are less predictable, ones that will be outlined later.

Moving to the left side we see factors related to a sizable market shift that are usually going to effect defined sectors of the stock market much more than the broad market as a whole. This goes back to classic supply and demand both in the realm of economics and in terms of stock pricing. For economics it is simply a kind of business that will decline due to a situation of decreasing demand and increasing supply. The chart of the Canadian markets in the mid 2010s seen in chapter 2 are examples of this. Resource based economies were facing a situation of lower demand while supply was proportionally more. As a result businesses and therefore stocks related to those businesses declined in value as investors pulled out due to poor prospects of growth. This then led to the stock pricing side of the matter. As soon as there were more sellers than buyers there were ideal conditions for SMCs as they caused a cascading effect. In addition after prices began to fall the full scope of such disparity between supply and demand became even more apparent from trends in production and logistics of resources. This then provided even more reason for investors to sell and drive the market lower.

The left and right branches both cover the general phenomenon of planned panic discussed earlier. Once stock markets reach certain tipping points it is possible for small drops to evolve into SMCs due to overreaction in the short term that is driven by the compounding effect such as the ones discussed above. Once the crowd that is the stock market begins to move it does so at an accelerated pace once expectations lean drastically towards a bearish outlook. In effect falling stock prices are driven by fundamental forces such as supply and demand of resources along with stagnation and contraction in the economy. This then gets compounded as stock prices fall which justify the initial fundamental reasoning further. SMCs can also begin on the technical side with charts displaying falling stock prices that then lead to justification with fundamental factors that in turn lead to more selling based on technical analysis of charts. However that is more common with the factors that are discussed next.

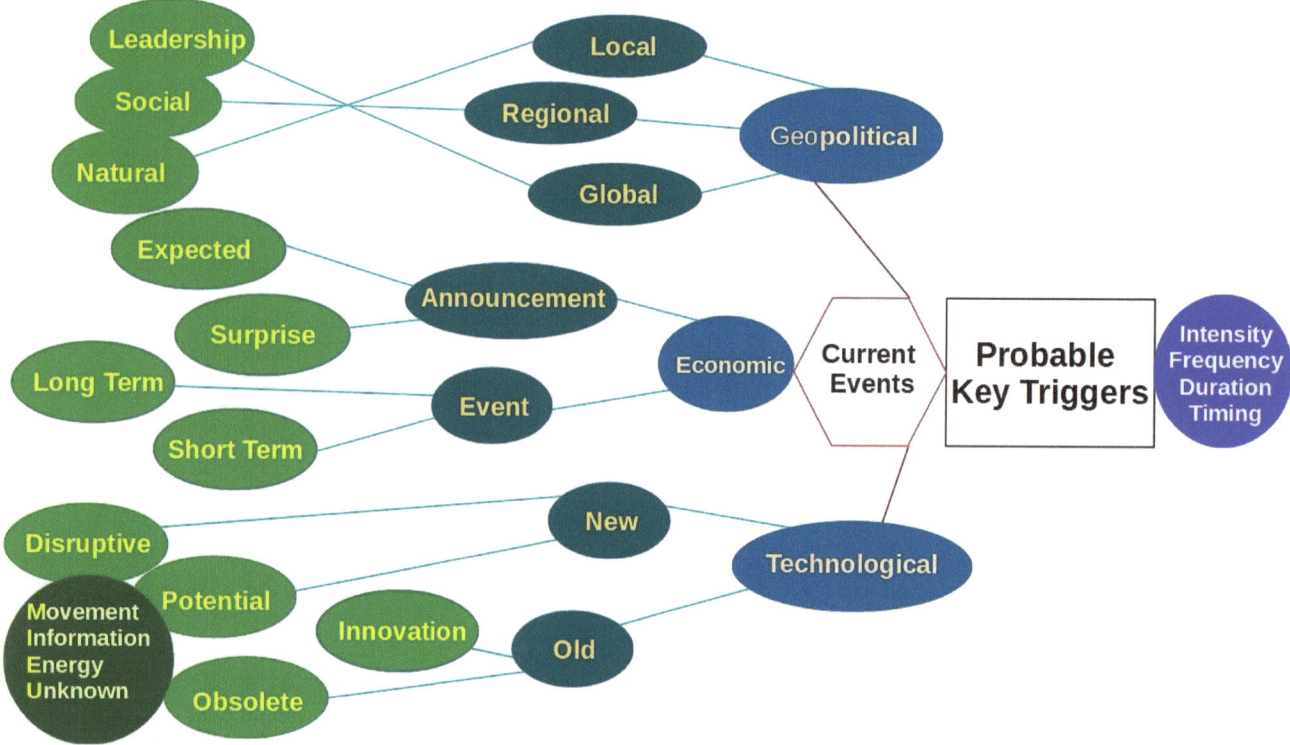

Figure 3.16

Figure 3.16 outlines the main categories and subcategories that can be classified as "Probable Key Triggers." These factors can be foreseen but to a lesser degree than what was outlined in figures 3.14 and 3.15. For example geopolitical factors are a common catalyst for driving markets. They can be events at the local level, but most often involve regional and global matters. That is why so much regular news is interrelated to happenings in the stock market on a regular basis.

Saying economic factors is a broad term would be an understatement, but like geopolitical factors it is a wide ranging area and the unique combination of influences present for each SMC can vary drastically. However it is important to note economic factors can range from the short term to long term impacts. Often short term impacts are more closely tied to sudden corrections that may even be called flash crashes. While more long term economic events are more closely related to the traditional SMC with at least a 20% drop lasting 6 months or more.

Economic events can be fully known about ahead of time, for example the date of the Brexit vote that was seen in chapter 2. This can also apply to other macro economic factors such as the change in leadership of a company, nation or major organization such as the World Health Organization. As well it can also be regular quarterly reports on a smaller scale for individual stocks or monthly employment reports. Events such as these can rock markets with short term volatility. This is even more applicable when economic announcements and events are a complete surprise. For example it can be a normal scheduled event such as an earnings report for a company or results for a national election. However if the outcome is not what the majority of the market expected, the disparity between reality and expectation can result in volatility which can contribute to an SMC if intensified for an extended time.

Technology always plays a factor in changing the world and the stock market is no different. Certain industries or an entire stock market can enter a prolonged bearish phase when certain technology has the potential to disrupt the existing order or the euphoria over a new technology has been overstated. The key word here is potential because the stock market is moved in part by prospective outcomes as was discussed in chapter 2 when comparing the economy and the stock market. Therefore a technology only needs to present possible change and not necessarily deliver. Some examples of this have been augmented and virtual reality which had very over stated expectations during the infancy of their development. Then to a lesser extent there was 3D entertainment technology and 3D printing which were initially similar with reality not living up to the hype, but eventually these technologies improved to become increasingly practical on a larger scale and presenting growing change to existing entertainment and manufacturing.

Then there is the concrete case of online retail which first started out as a small portion of retail during the inception of the internet. However as the early 21st century moved on the online retail space became a dominant force with reality far exceeding potential expectations. This classic example reshaped the retail landscape with old brick and mortar stores adapting or going extinct while strict online retailers increased at a rapid rate. While this didn't impact stock markets on a broad scale it did crash the old order of retail stocks and left a few old companies standing alongside the stocks of pioneering online retailers.

Additionally the innovation around automation has always been a driving force in changing the economy and the stock market. Like the example of retail old industries that don't adapt will eventually fall out of existence as they hold on to obsolete technology. It is difficult for the general public and the majority of market participants to determine which new technologies will impact the world and the markets. However if history is any indication any advancement in information and energy transportation are bound to have far ranging implications for the broad markets.

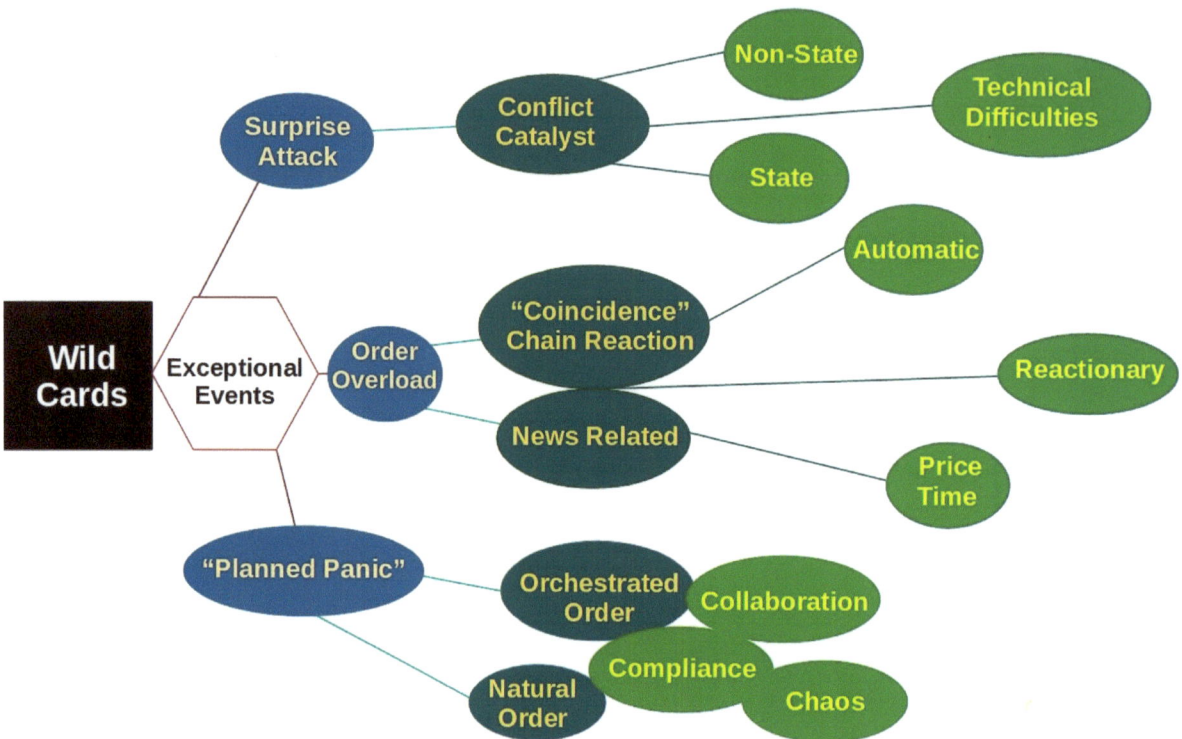

Figure 3.17

Figure 3.17 outlines the main categories and subcategories that can be classified as "Wild Cards." These are virtually unpredictable and unforeseeable influences contributing to SMCs. Falling stock prices can literally be the result of surprise attacks that are essentially catalysts for conflict. This refers to any event that is perceived as an attack that involves state and/or non-state actors. Most often this conjures up images of national armies and terrorist groups conducting physical attacks however it can also involve cyber attacks from hacking or mere uttering of threats with no action.

It is not so much the attacks themselves that cause SMCs. They are more in the realm of peripheral factors that cause uncertainty and contribute to an SMC or accelerate an existing decline into a further SMC. The 9/11 attacks were one such example where an already bearish market was lowered even more. As well such factors also result in small to medium price drops from time to time when international tensions rise over actual minor attacks or threats of attack that have the potential to escalate into major conflict. These are more common and don't lead to full scale war of any kind but they increase short term volatility and produce some major short term drops from time to time. Some examples of this often occurred when shipping routes around the middle east and Africa were disrupted by violent or threatening incidences. As well as the periodic missile testing from North Korea during their early nuclear programs.

Exceptional events often result in "order overload" which involves high amounts of sell orders that can put a market into panic. These can be driven purely by technical structures on stock charts and they are most commonly explained by new catalysts which are essentially any major news events that can negatively impact the markets. Such surges in short term selling often begin for less than a day and can be unintentional and/or planned manipulation of stock prices. News releases of events like the ones discussed above are merely the tipping point or justification used to initiate a first spike in sell orders that usually drives the market down further as fear sets in. This is an extremely broad area and can even cover events such as natural disasters and pandemics that present a negative outlook for future growth. In any case SMCs originating from news catalysts are automatic to some degree because as discussed earlier there will be traders and investors who already plan to sell ahead of time in the case certain supporting price ranges are breached. As well there are also automatic algorithms that exist with a similar purpose in order to decrease losses during the rapid first stage of an SMC. Then there are the reactionary sellers who take part in the "planned panic" and begin selling due to crowd behavior over the fear of losing more as the market continues to drop. Lastly the market can simply continue to fall based on technical factors on stock charts that originate from chart patterns and intervals that are characteristic of up trends in the process of correcting.

Finally there is the ambiguous area regarding a discussion of market manipulation and natural order. Stock markets can crash naturally and they can be manipulated. The answer is never so clear cut. It is often a mix of the two and it is difficult to prove either one. Largely because stock prices can naturally fall and there is always interest to have markets fall. SMCs can be theoretically be engineered with orchestrated price drops. These might not even make up the bulk of falling price but they initiate a cascading effect of further selling that can be the result of collaboration and/or compliance of the market to sell off in a semi natural fashion. For as we have seen and discussed SMCs only need certain thresholds to be crossed at the beginning to turn small to medium sized price drops/corrections into full blown SMCs. Manipulators only need to get the ball rolling to push the market on the desired downward slope, and not actually take part in the majority of selling. The idea for manipulation is straightforward enough, a desired bearish outcome needs to incite the crowd behavior to quickly sell. However due to the dynamic nature of stock markets it can be difficult if not impossible to fully prove cases of manipulation that lead to SMCs.

Figure 3.18

Flash crashes have already been discussed in chapter two and there is not much more to say about them. The important note is to remember the rarity of them as an anomaly that may never be fully explained.

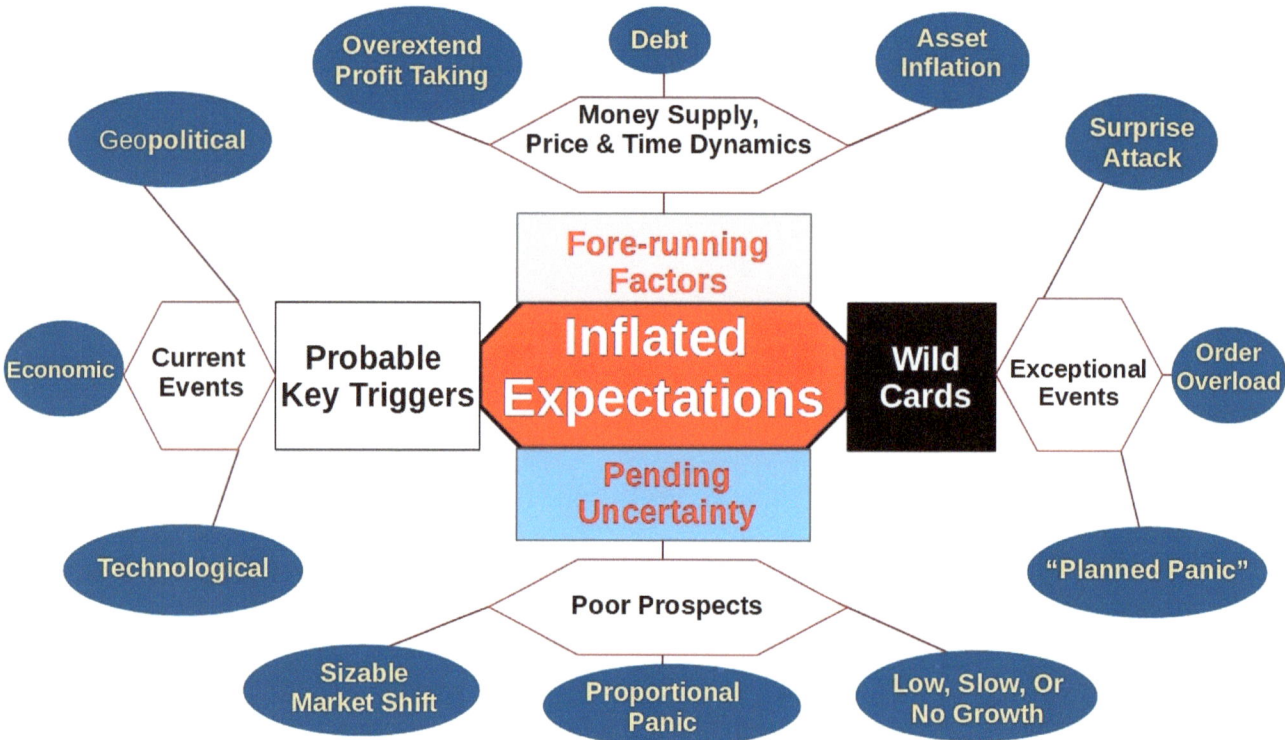

Figure 3.19

With all the varying and dynamic factors behind SMCs it is no wonder technical analysis of charts provides an excellent summary of diverse events in the form of relatively simple price action.

Chapter 4

Stock Market Crash Strategies

Figure 4.0

Now that the context and characteristics of SMCs have been covered it is time to discuss methods of mitigating the impact of SMCs to reduce losses and even increase profits. Though before outlining the methods it is crucial to have realistic expectations, especially to accept that losses can be reduced but there will still be heightened risk during an SMC. Also there are lots and lots of strategies and it is not possible or wise to use all of them simultaneously.

The following strategies are applicable to cases from a single stock dropping and an entire economic sector falling, to a recession and full stock market crash. Not all strategies are appropriate for all scenarios. People usually pick one or a few. Rarely if ever are all the strategies used at once successfully because they require special knowledge and skill to use. In some instances strategies may contradict each other too. Should you decide to educate yourself further it is best to pick one topic at a time, learn it well, practice it, then apply it on a small scale first. No matter which method it is, each one can be applied more effectively with proficient skill in price and time analysis of stock charts.

Strategy 1

Increase Cash Reserves

This is exactly what it sounds like. It means directing a greater portion of wealth into cash. This can be done through several ways.

- Direct free "cash flow" (ex: dividend payments, interest, extra savings) into cash or cash equivalents such as short term bonds, treasury bills, or money market funds.
- Cash out the riskier portions of a portfolio. Sell stocks in riskier/more volatile sectors and hold the cash. Essentially converting risky assets into cash.

(+) Cash is on the lower end of the risk scale. It generally declines in value stably and predictably. It is appropriate for short term down turns and would only really loose significant value quickly in less than one year in extremely rare cases of hyper inflation.

(-) Cash just declines in value as time goes on, due to inflation.
There is low to no potential for an increase in wealth by simply holding cash.

(+) Holding cash allows for more **flexibility** to sit and wait for opportunities to buy into whatever asset you choose when the opportunity is right. For example buying stocks, real-estate, or commodities after they have significantly decreased in value and have begun a stable recovery.

Strategy 2

Moving To "Defensive" Stocks

The word "defensive" is often used to describe stocks that are said to be more stable. They are usually the stocks of long established companies that pay dividends. As a result the prices of such stocks often decrease at a slower rate compared to the rest of the stock market during an SMC.

(+) Avoiding the less stable stocks in less essential sectors lowers the risk of a greater drop in overall portfolio value.

(-) This is not a 100% safe route away from risk. The overall market is dropping but the portfolio will drop less since it is out of the faster falling sectors.

(+) Cash from the sale of riskier stocks can go towards increasing cash reserves and/or towards reallocation to the "safer"/"defensive" stocks. Cash is also normally generated from dividends in the "safer" sectors since they are often businesses with lots of physical assets and cash flow. Dividends could still be paid or paid at a reduced rate if they are not temporarily halted during a market downturn.

(-) "Defensive stocks" can still fail if the companies are operating poorly. They offer a false sense of security. Investors and traders must still be vigilant about which "defensive stocks" they pick and when they buy them. Leaving cash in such stocks can lead to missed opportunities if cash is tied up in them instead of just holding cash, which is more liquid and can quickly be deployed to buy stocks and other assets when there is opportunity.

(-) Normally "defensive stocks" are confined to a few sectors such as the consumer staples sector, thereby limiting the diversification possibilities to an extent. There will be a lower variety of sectors and stocks to choose from as a consequence which may be a negative aspect if an investor has the goal of greater diversification in their stock holdings.

Strategy 3

Diversifying To Assets Outside The Stock Market

In the case of downtrends of individual stocks and sectors or even recessions, assets outside the stock market may be unaffected or less affected by the down turn. The number one asset outside the stock market has historically been gold followed by silver and other precious metals such as platinum. Gold and other precious metals tend to retain their value better even during recessions and stock market crashes. Mainly because they are rarer physical assets. Gold sometimes has an inverse relation to the stock market as it goes up in price when stocks go down. This is because they are one of the first assets cash gets moved to out of fear of a falling stock market. Though keep in mind it is a correlational relationship not a causal one. Moreover the correlation between stock prices falling and gold price rising and visa versa is dynamic and changes in strength all the time.

(+) Gold and other precious metals are more a counter or hedge to protect against down markets. They are similar to cash in terms of being more stable and having lower volatility compared to stocks during SMCs. However they aren't a common way to rapidly grow wealth even though they can see price surges from time to time. Investing in gold and other assets outside the stock market requires additional knowledge and skill to be done effectively similar to developing the skill and knowledge to effectively trade and invest different types of stocks, sectors, and time frames in the stock market.

(-) Like cash and "defensive stocks" gold and precious metals can lead to a false sense of security. They are not 100% safe. Just look at past downtrends, recessions, and stock market crashes. They still generally drop in price albeit normally not as much as the stock market. Moreover other assets such as currency and real-estate present their own set of risk factors depending on what is behind a particular SMC. For as we have seen the merging of multiple market forces such as falling resource prices and real-estate prices can be heavily linked to SMCs. There is definitely potential in other markets but it comes at a price of additional layers of complexity.

Strategy 4

Short Selling

Shorting stocks can allow for profit potential when stocks decrease in value. A quick summary of shorting is: the immediate selling of a stock on margin(basically borrowed money/shares by the broker) Profits are made when the stock drops and it is bought back at a lower price.

(+) Allows for profits to be gained from falling stock prices. Relatively straightforward concept after an initial learning curb.

(-) High risk and high potential for losses especially if the margin is high or even leveraged at a 2x, 3x, or higher rate.

(-) Only a short term strategy to protect or profit, not a viable long term strategy or even medium term method in most cases.

(-) Still the risk of loosing in the event the market is not dropping enough and continues higher. Greater potential for more losses since upside movement is theoretically infinite versus a traditional long position that can only drop to zero with 100% losses. Shorting can theoretically lead to 100% or greater losses. For example a stock is shorted at a price of $70. This means shares of the stock are technically immediately borrowed and sold at $70. A drop of $15 taking the stock price down to $55 results in the short position becoming profitable by $15. The maximum the stock can drop is to $0. However the maximum price the stock can rise to is unlimited. It can rise to $80 for a $10 loss on each share. To $100, $170, $250 and so on. The loss potential can far exceed 100% and there have been plenty of cases where stocks continue on such a rise. That is why such a strategy is only suitable for the initial rapid phases of an SMC and not a long term holding that would be more appropriate with a dividend stock for example.

Strategy 5

Inverse ETFs

Inverse ETFs are Exchange Traded Funds that replicate the inverse movements of the market and certain economic sectors. They use derivatives, shorting, and other methods to achieve an inverse movement in price in relation to the stock market or a particular sector they are meant to track. For example thicker symbol "DOG" ETF is meant to perform the exact opposite of the normal Dow index.

(+) Allow for profiting from downside movements of broad stock market indices and sectors.

(-) Are "artificial" representations of price. To achieve inverse price movements inverse ETFs are not true representations of any one tangible asset.

(-) In the case of regular 1x inverse ETFs there are the same risks as mentioned before with shorting. With 2x or higher leveraged inverse ETFs there is the added risk of margin and greater than 100% potential loss also mentioned earlier with shorting.

Strategy 6

Avoiding Margin

This is simple avoid borrowing of any kind

Don't Buy On Margin
Don't Finance Real Estate With Mortgages
Don't Spend More Than You Can Afford
Don't Purchase Everything With Credit Cards

This seems like a no brainer but they are big mistakes even when there is no stock market downturn. Simply follow the old adage and never invest more than you are willing to lose. Don't invest with money that isn't yours.

Strategy 7

Maximizing Value Buying And Avoiding Buying Traps

Whether it is an individual stock that has been oversold, or an entire class of assets that has hit the proverbial bottom, all should be careful of buying in at the wrong time. Of course it is impossible to always buy stocks on the cheap at the exact right time. What we can do is follow some basic principles to at least buy value at more appropriate times and increase the chances of avoiding false bottoms. There will still be risk for further price drops and even losses but such steps reduce the frequency of making mistakes. (build skill with price and time analysis of stock charts to better prepare)

- Be patient don't buy right when there is a drop. Large drops of a single stock or whole market crash usually have the bulk of the drop(estimated 20-60%) of lost value in the first 1/3-1/2 of the down slide in price. These are just rough metrics but generally apply to most large stock drops. Just reference past stock slumps and market crashes to see. This refers to the first few phases of an SMC that were discussed and demonstrated in chapter 2. Watch those first key support ranges very carefully once they begin to develop after the initial rapid drop.

- Scale in and buy shares at different points in time to spread out risk. This will reduce the chances of dumping all your money at the wrong time. You will miss some opportunity if it is the exact bottom but you will also miss loosing large sums when there are false bottoms and temporary bounces.

- Don't become too attached to a stock or sector. Even a "safe" stock that seems like it has solid business can't retain all its value when the broader stock market & macro economic factors are selling off. The business is good but conditions of the market and time are not.

Strategy 8

Staying Disciplined For A Long Term Perspective

In order to survive a stock market crash or smaller downturn it is important to stay disciplined and keep a long term perspective for all strategies to work, especially the previous one. Below is an age old tip to keep it together while the market declines. Be patient and don't check the news too often and glue your eyes to your portfolio and stock charts. Even a temporary price drop for a single stock takes time. Don't damage your psychological well-being over what you can't control.

Strategy 9

Stock Options

Stock options can allow for profiting from neutral and downward price movement too. They carry many of the same risks as shorting if done wrong but can be much more flexible than any other strategy if managed right. This comes at the price of a **steep learning curve and high losses** when options are used without the proper knowledge and experience. The following are a few options strategies for down markets. It is highly recommended to have a solid foundation of knowledge of stock options before learning about individual strategies such as the following. Learn and practice each strategy to understand the concepts behind their potential profit and more importantly risk profiles. Only then is it suitable to try them in real live markets in small increments first.

- Protective Puts
- Covered Calls (only for stocks that will be held for the long term)
- Collar
- Skewed Iron Condors or Skewed Butterfly spreads
- Broken Wing Butterfly Spread

Strategy 10

Control Spending

This last strategy is common sense but it is followed by very few even during good economic times. Here are a few tips that will help anytime especially during a declining stock market.

- Avoid over spending and using margin and credit
- Delay big purchases
- Avoid unnecessary spending, especially on items just for show.
- Create a budget and stick to it, nobody will judge you for being cheap, especially during a recession when everybody needs to reduce spending.
- Avoid instant gratification to build patience

Hopefully you now have a better understanding of SMCs and what can be done during times of decline in the stock market. Remember to keep practicing those charting skills and be alert to factors that can contribute to SMCs.

All the best and take care.

For more on trading, charting, and the markets visit www.ascencore.com/

www.ingramcontent.com/pod-product-compliance
Lightning Source LLC
Chambersburg PA
CBHW041932240526
45473CB00034B/928